Andrea & Bob

Congratulations on your Wedding
and Best wishes for the future.

Jane & Ted

September 28th 1996

THE CONRAN COOKBOOKS

ONE-COURSE FEASTS

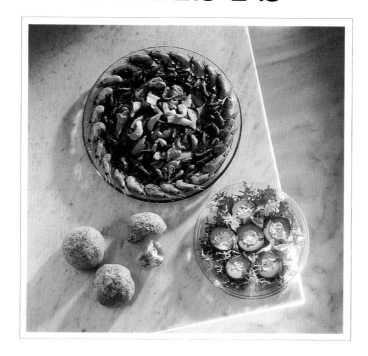

COLIN SPENCER

CONRAN OCTOPUS

This edition published in 1991 by
Conran Octopus Limited
37 Shelton Street
London WC2H 9HN

First published in 1986

Photographer Laurie Evans
Editorial Consultant Caro Hobhouse
House Editor Susie Ward
Art Director Douglas Wilson
Art Editor Clive Hayball
Photographic Art Direction Valerie Wright Heneghan
Home Economist Michel Thomson
Photographic Stylist Leslie Evans
Art Assistant Nina Thomas

ISBN 1 85029 354 6

The publishers would like to thank the following
for their assistance with photographic props:
Heal's, 196 Tottenham Court Road, London W1;
The Conran Shop, Fulham Road, London SW3;
Habitat Designs Limited

Title page: Marinated Fish Salad, Sliced Stuffed Avocado,
Celery Herb Rolls (page 20-22)

Typeset by SX Composing, Essex
Printed and bound in China

CONTENTS

INTRODUCTION

Most people feel easier if principles are clearly delineated in black and white terms, so that one is either vegetarian or a meat eater. However, one can have strong principles without falling into an obvious camp. Good food, it seems to me, should be good in more than one sense of the word. Seen in very general terms, why should the food we eat either exploit the labourer who grows it or rape the land? Good food is also concerned with the living conditions of the animal, and must necessarily bestow health and well-being upon us rather than harm our bodies. Last – but not least – the food should be good in the sense in which it is most commonly used – imaginative, pleasing to the eye, with an enticing elegance and style which make it more than simply palatable. All this may seem a tall order. But I believe it is quite possible to steer a delicate course along these principles.

Even if an ethical stance does not appeal to you, it is wise for reasons of health to follow a diet of chiefly vegetables with a little fish and game. I avoid all factory-farmed meat and fowl like the plague; I loathe the barbaric conditions of these animals' lives and slaughter, and the chemical additives and the growth hormones in their feed are also a health hazard to humans. I do eat the occasional game bird in season. The wilder it is, the better it tastes and the healthier it is for you to consume since its fat content is minimal: an animal living off a diet foraged in natural surroundings produces three times as much protein as fat, while factory-farmed animals produce three times as much fat as protein. I also think a little fish is beneficial for general health. Fish are high in polyunsaturated oils. However, farmed fish, too, are much fattier and should be avoided whenever possible.

I have divided the book up into seasons – because seasonal food, bought when it is at its peak and as fresh as possible, will have more flavour as well as be more nutritious. And I have presented the recipes as a series of menus in which two or three dishes complement each other to provide a balanced meal that looks as good as it tastes. A salad, however simple, should accompany them, or be eaten afterwards to refresh the palate. Most of these menus have been devised for special occasions but you can, of course, swap and substitute many of the dishes to make a less extravagant meal.

I think that the food in this book, which embraces all the current health edicts, is fairly uncomplicated and trouble free, yet will appeal to all the finer senses of a dedicated gastronome.

Colin Spencer

SPRING

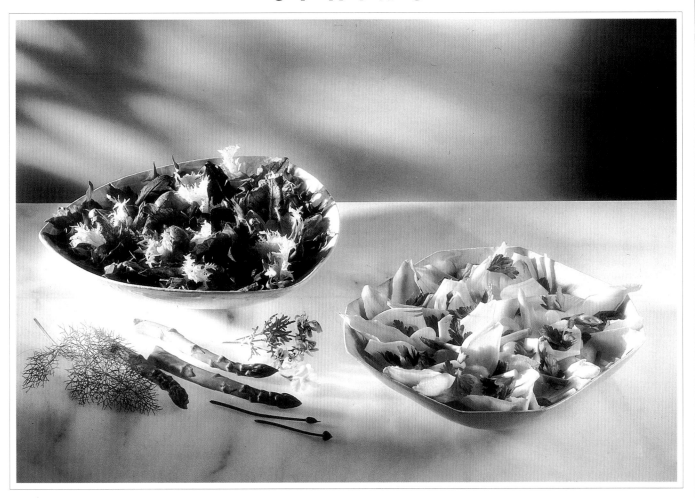

The most exciting spring salads are green and leafy. Young dandelion or spinach leaves, and the seedling thinnings of peppery rocket, radicchio, chicory, endive and lettuce (sold in the French markets under the name of *mesclun*), are all rich in vitamin C and delicious tossed *au naturel* with the most simple of dressings. Watercress is also at its best, chicory and endive make their first appearance, and the first shoots of fennel, lovage, parsley and sorrel can be picked in the kitchen-garden.

SPRING · MENU 1

SHELLFISH ROULADE

•

SPINACH MOULDS IN SORREL SAUCE

•

BAKED FENNEL

This is a fairly sumptuous meal and there are snobs among us who would complain at the baking of oysters at all. But the plump Pacific oyster cooks beautifully and flavours the wholemeal puff pastry from within. Mussels may be substituted if oysters are not available.

The pastry will not rise as eloquently as puff pastry made from all white flour but it will taste much nicer and have a speckled crust to it. Present the finished roulade on a platter garnished with some of the raw feathery fronds of the fennel.

The spinach, sorrel and fennel, which are good foils to the richness of the roulade, should be served separately because of their individual sauces.

But for the pastry, this is a meal with little carbohydrate in it. It was planned in my mind for an early spring day when one yearns for the lighter food of summer so I believe that it might not be a bad thing to have a salad made from rice mixed with every possible fresh herb you could then lay your hands on.

Left to right: Spinach Mould in Sorrel Sauce (page 8), Baked Fennel (page 9), Shellfish Roulade (page 8).

SHELLFISH ROULADE

Illustrated on pages 6-7

—————— SERVES 6 ——————

12 Pacific oysters or 36 mussels
5 oz (140 g) curd cheese
1 bunch spring onions, finely chopped
2 tablespoons double cream
2 tablespoons grated Gruyère cheese
sea salt and freshly ground black pepper
butter for greasing
for the pastry
6 oz (170 g) plain flour
2 oz (50 g) wholemeal flour
pinch of salt
2 teaspoons baking powder
7 oz (200 g) butter
lemon juice
1 egg, beaten
2 tablespoons toasted sesame seeds
a little plain flour for dusting

———————————————————

To make the pastry, sift the flours into a mixing bowl with the salt and baking powder and add the bran in the sieve. Divide the butter into 3 equal pieces. Rub one piece of butter into the flour, using the fingertips, add the lemon juice and a little water, if necessary, to make a dough. Roll out on a floured board. Dice the remaining butter and scatter half of it across the pastry. Fold the outside edges of the pastry over to make an envelope, roll out into a rectangle and repeat the process with the remaining butter. Fold in the sides and roll out. Continue folding and rolling until the pastry is firm and pliable. If it gets sticky, chill in the refrigerator for 30 minutes and then continue. Finally roll out to a square roughly 12×12 in (30×30 cm). Heat the oven to 425°F (220°C, gas mark 7).

Extract the oyster meats from their shells and place in a mixing bowl. Add the curd cheese, onions, cream, Gruyère and salt and pepper to taste. Mix thoroughly and spread the mixture over the pastry, leaving a 1-in

(2.5-cm) border round the edges. If using mussels, discard any which are open, then steam the rest briefly until they all open. Extract the mussel meats and place in a mixing bowl, adding the other ingredients as above.

Roll up the pastry carefully and press down the ends, brushing with a little egg to seal firmly. Lay the roulade seam-side down on a well-buttered baking tray. Brush beaten egg over the surface and sprinkle with the sesame seeds. Bake for 25-30 minutes, until the roulade is puffed up and golden. Transfer to a serving platter and serve cut into slices.

SPINACH MOULDS
IN SORREL SAUCE

Illustrated on pages 6/7

—————— SERVES 6 ——————

1½ lb (675 g) spinach leaves, stalks and coarse ribs removed
2 oz (50 g) butter
1 tablespoon split pea flour
3 tablespoons grated Gruyère cheese
1 tablespoon freshly grated Parmesan cheese
2 eggs, beaten
sea salt and freshly ground black pepper
butter for greasing
for the sauce
1 lb (450 g) sorrel leaves
½ pint (280 ml) plain yoghurt
sea salt and freshly ground black pepper

———————————————————

Cook the spinach in the butter in a heavy saucepan over a low heat for 10 minutes, or until tender. Break it up with a wooden spoon until reduced to a coarse purée. Add the flour and cook briefly until thickened. Add the cheeses and stir until just melted, then remove from the heat and mix in the eggs and salt and pepper to taste.

Heat the oven to 400°F (200°C, gas mark 6).

Butter 6 individual dariole moulds and fill two-thirds full with the spinach mixture. Bake for 12-15 minutes or until risen.

Meanwhile, wash the sorrel and tear the leaves from the stalks, place in a heavy saucepan without water or butter and cook over a low heat for 3 minutes. Break up the leaves with a wooden spoon as above, then add the yoghurt, stir well to make a smooth sauce and simmer very gently for 1-2 minutes. Season to taste with salt and pepper.

Turn out the moulds on to a serving dish or individual plates and pour the sauce around them.

BAKED FENNEL

Illustrated on pages 6/7

─────── SERVES 6 ───────

4 bulbs fennel
2 oz (50 g) butter
finely grated zest and juice of 1 lemon
4 fl oz (110 ml) dry white vermouth
sea salt and freshly ground black pepper

Heat the oven to 375°F (190°C, gas mark 5).

Trim and quarter the fennel bulbs.

In a large oven- and flameproof dish, melt the butter with the lemon zest and juice over a gentle heat. Lay the pieces of fennel in it. Pour over the vermouth and season to taste with salt and pepper. Bring to simmering point, then bake in the oven for 30 minutes.

Transfer the fennel to a heated serving dish and pour over the sauce.

SPRING · MENU 2

LOTTE AND SCAMPI TIMBALE WITH A CRAB SAUCE

•

NEW POTATOES WITH GREEN PEPPERCORNS

•

STUFFED CUCUMBERS

There is public confusion over the monkfish. Two fish are commonly called monkfish and only one is eaten in large numbers, but the one that is eaten is not the one that is photographed or illustrated in fish and cookery books. The tail of the angler fish (lotte in French) is the fish we eat – 500,000 tons of it in Europe each year. The other fish – the angel fish or shark (ange de mer) – can be found in fish markets very occasionally. Fishmongers sell the first, while having the second illustrated on their walls.

I have specified scampi tails because, for this dish, you must have raw scampi. It can be bought frozen and will have more flavour than the boiled scampi in their shells. If whole shellfish are not cooked immediately, the toxins in the head will contaminate the whole fish. This is why raw shellfish are sold without their heads.

It may seem odd to combine the angler fish and scampi, as they taste similar, but there are differences in flavour which are noticeable in this dish, and they blend beautifully with the crab sauce.

The whole dish can be prepared beforehand and then cooked in a bain marie at the last moment. Both cucumber and new potatoes are particularly good with fish. Indeed, they have become classic accompaniments. The stuffed cucumbers can be prepared earlier and their final baking done just before you need them. The potatoes should be cooked at the last moment.

Clockwise from top: New Potatoes with Green Peppercorns, Lotte and Scampi Timbale, Stuffed Cucumbers.

LOTTE AND SCAMPI TIMBALE

— SERVES 6 —

1½ lb (675 g) lotte (usually sold as monkfish, chopped)
1 lb (450 g) scampi tails, chopped
plain flour for dusting
2 oz (50 g) butter
½ pint (280 ml) dry white wine
½ pint (280 ml) milk
a generous handful of parsley, finely chopped
sea salt and freshly ground black pepper
2 eggs, beaten
butter for greasing
for the sauce
brown and white meat from 2 crabs
¼ pint (150 ml) dry white wine
1 oz (25 g) butter
1 tablespoon plain flour
½ pint (280 ml) plain yoghurt
3 fl oz (80 ml) brandy

Heat the oven to 400°F (200°C, gas mark 6).

Roll the chopped lotte and scampi in flour.

Melt the butter in a heavy frying pan, add the fish and fry briefly for 2 minutes, then add the wine, milk, parsley and salt and pepper to taste. Mix thoroughly and immediately remove from the heat before it can even simmer. Allow to cool slightly, then stir in the eggs.

Butter a 2½-pint (1.4-litre) soufflé dish and pour the fish mixture into it. Place in a bain marie and bake for 30 minutes, or until a knife inserted into it comes out clean. Remove from the oven and set aside for 8 minutes.

Meanwhile, make the sauce. Place the crabmeat in a blender or food processor with the wine and brandy. Reduce to a purée. Melt the butter in a saucepan, blend in the flour and cook for 1 minute, stirring. Pour in the crab purée, then add the yoghurt and salt and pepper to taste. Stir over a very gentle heat to make a smooth sauce, then remove from the heat. Unmould the timbale on to a large platter and pour the sauce around it.

STUFFED CUCUMBERS

— SERVES 6 —

2 cucumbers
2 oz (50 g) butter
2 bunches spring onions, sliced
a large bunch of parsley, chopped
2 oz (50 g) Gruyère cheese, grated
1 oz (25 g) freshly grated Parmesan
sea salt and freshly ground black pepper

Peel the cucumbers in strips to give a striped effect. Cut them crossways into 4-in (10-cm) pieces. Scoop out and discard all the seeds. Boil the cucumber pieces in salted water for 4 minutes, then drain well and pat dry.

Heat the oven to 400°F (200°C, gas mark 6).

Heat the butter in a frying pan and fry the spring onions until soft. Remove from the heat, cool, and mix in the remaining ingredients.

Spoon the mixture into each cucumber piece. Place the pieces in a buttered ovenproof dish and bake in the oven for 15 minutes.

NEW POTATOES WITH GREEN PEPPERCORNS

— SERVES 6 —

New potatoes, to which we so look forward every spring, can benefit from more than a pat of butter.

For every pound of new potatoes (for six people you will need 2 lbs), melt 1½ tablespoons of olive oil and a tablespoon of butter in a heavy saucepan. Add the potatoes and sprinkle with a teaspoon of green peppercorns. Cover and simmer for 10-15 minutes, shaking frequently. Then add another teaspoon of peppercorns, salt to taste and a tablespoon of breadcrumbs. Cook for another 8 minutes or so, then transfer to a heat-proof dish, brown under a grill, scatter attractively with parsley, and serve.

SPRING · MENU 3

SWEET POTATO AND OKRA CURRY
·
MILD MUSHROOM AND CELERIAC CURRY
·
BUCKWHEAT AND ADUKI BEAN PILAF

Here are two spiced dishes in which the spices are both subtle and fiery. They go with an unusual pilaf which has the sharpness of redcurrants added to it.

Okra is a vegetable which some people are nervous of because, without being warned beforehand, they discover its mucilaginous quality. This is invaluable in the cooking and gives the texture to what we know as gumbos. But the okra must not be cut into to expose its seeds before it is cooked, so merely trim the stalk and never slice into the top of the vegetable.

Curries and fruit, as we have learned from India, combine well together and the sharper the fruit, the more it cleanses the palate. In India they use the fresh tamarind pulp, but in late spring we have the benefit of all our own varieties of soft fruit.

Like all spice dishes, these curries are better if they are cooked the day before, for then the spices have the time to permeate the whole dish. The pilaf can also be prepared in advance, but add the fruit at the last moment. If there are no redcurrants available, use early cherries, stoned and chopped.

SWEET POTATO AND OKRA CURRY

——— SERVES 6 ———

1½ lb (675 g) sweet potato, thickly sliced
½ lb (225 g) okra, trimmed
2 onions, sliced
3 tablespoons ghee or corn oil
2 oz (50 g) ginger root, thinly sliced
3 cardamoms, black seeds crushed
2 dried red chillies, crushed
2 teaspoons mustard seeds
1 teaspoon each ground cumin, coriander, turmeric and fenugreek
1 tablespoon chopped coriander leaves

Heat the ghee in a large saucepan, add the ginger and all the spices, and cook for 1 minute. Add the sweet potatoes, okra and onions and stir. Bring to simmering point, then cover and cook for a further 15 minutes. Stir in the coriander leaves and transfer to a heated serving dish.

MILD MUSHROOM AND CELERIAC CURRY

——— SERVES 6 ———

3 small celeriac, peeled and chopped
1 lb (450 g) mushrooms, sliced
2 tablespoons ghee or corn oil
2 tablespoons asafoetida
a small piece each of tamarind, mace and cassia
finely grated zest and juice of 2 lemons
7 fl oz (200 ml) plain yoghurt
sea salt

Heat the ghee in a large saucepan and add the spices. Cook for 1 minute, then add the celeriac and mushrooms. Stir and shake the pan. Add the lemon zest >

Clockwise, from left: Buckwheat and Aduki Bean Pilaf (page 14); Mild Mushroom and Celeriac Curry; Sweet Potato and Okra Curry.

< and juice, cover and simmer for 10 minutes. Now add the yoghurt and a pinch of salt. Cook uncovered for a further 10 minutes, then transfer to a heated serving dish.

BUCKWHEAT AND ADUKI BEAN PILAF

Illustrated on page 10

―――――――――― SERVES 6 ――――――――――

3 oz (85 g) aduki beans
3 oz (85 g) buckwheat
sea salt and freshly ground black pepper
4 oz (120 g) redcurrants, off their stalks

Soak the beans for 1 hour. Cover and simmer in the soaking water for 45-60 minutes, topping up with extra boiling water, if necessary, until tender. If there is any water left, drain thoroughly.

Simmer the buckwheat in a little salted water for 10 minutes, until all the liquid is absorbed. Add the beans and salt and pepper to taste. Mix thoroughly.

Just before serving, stir in the redcurrants, then transfer to a heated serving dish.

Clockwise, from top left; Devilled Vegetable Pie (page 16); Potato Gratin with Chèvre (page 16); Leeks stuffed with Mange-tout Purée.

SPRING · MENU 4
·

LEEKS STUFFED
WITH MANGE-TOUT PUREE

POTATO GRATIN WITH CHEVRE

DEVILLED VEGETABLE PIE

The attractive quality of all pies is that they can be made the day before and then reheated. They are probably better for this, especially this one which has so many spices in the sauce. The gratin made with chèvre (goat's cheese) has a characteristic, earthy tang, and mange-tout and leeks are a lovely combination. Serve them on a small platter, for the gratin and the pie will be in their cooking dishes.

This particular menu demands at this time of year one of my favourite green salads – dandelion and rocket.

LEEKS STUFFED WITH MANGE-TOUT PUREE

——————— SERVES 6 ———————

6 fat leeks
½ lb (225 g) mange-tout
3 oz (85 g) butter
sea salt and freshly ground black pepper
¼ pint (150 ml) dry white wine

Trim away and discard the green parts of the leeks and clean the rest thoroughly. Take about 6 in (15 cm) of the white ends and slice in half crossways. From >

< each half cut a boat-shaped hollow. Chop up the leek you have cut out, melt 2 oz (50 g) of the butter and cook the chopped leek over a gentle heat until soft.

Meanwhile, trim the mange-tout and lightly boil them in a little salted water for 5 minutes, while steaming the hollowed-out leeks above them. The leeks are ready when still al dente and holding their shape.

Heat the oven to 425°F (220°C, gas mark 7).

Drain the mange-tout, transfer them to a blender or food processor and reduce to a purée. Add the chopped leeks with the butter, season to taste and blend again. Drain the steamed leeks and pat dry with kitchen paper. Fill them with the mange-tout and leek purée. Pour the wine into a shallow ovenproof dish. Lay the stuffed leeks in it, dot with the remaining butter and bake in the oven for 10 minutes.

POTATO GRATIN WITH CHEVRE

Illustrated on pages 14/15

SERVES 6

1½ lb (675 g) potatoes
4 oz (120 g) chèvre
1 oz (25 g) butter
sea salt and freshly ground black pepper
½ pint (300 ml) single cream

Peel and slice the potatoes thinly. Soak them in cold water for 1 hour, then drain and pat dry with kitchen paper. Use half of the butter to generously grease a shallow ovenproof dish. Cut the rind off the chèvre and slice the cheese thinly.

Heat the oven to 350°F (180°C, gas mark 4).

Layer the potato slices and chèvre in the dish, seasoning with salt and pepper and finishing with a layer of potato. Pour the cream over the top and dot with the remaining butter. Bake in the oven for 2 hours. Cover with a piece of foil if the top shows signs of overbrowning or drying out.

DEVILLED VEGETABLE PIE

Illustrated on page 14/15

SERVES 6
---

3 oz (85 g) chickpeas, soaked overnight
1 medium cauliflower, broken into florets
2 tablespoons olive oil
½ teaspoon each asafoetida and mustard seeds
1 oz (25 g) fresh ginger root, grated
2 onions, chopped
2 cloves garlic, chopped
10 fl oz (280 ml) red wine
2 tablespoons shoyu (Japanese soya) sauce
2 tablespoons moutarde de Meaux
for the pastry
4 oz (120 g) wholemeal flour
2 oz (50 g) butter
½ teaspoon salt
1 tablespoon lemon juice
beaten egg for glazing

Drain the chickpeas, then boil for 2 hours, covered, in plenty of fresh water, until tender. Drain and roughly crush half of them, leaving the rest whole. Reserve. Boil the cauliflower florets in salted water for 4 minutes, drain and reserve. Combine the two vegetables.

Sift the flour into a mixing bowl. Grate in the butter, add the salt and rub with the fingertips until the mixture resembles dry breadcrumbs. Add the lemon juice and mix to a dough. Chill in the refrigerator for 1 hour. Return to near room temperature and, between clingfilm, roll out to fit the top of your pie dish.

Heat the oven to 400°F (200°C, gas mark 6).

Heat the oil in a large saucepan and add the asafoetida, mustard seeds, ginger root, garlic and onions. Cook for 4-5 minutes until the onions begin to soften. Add the wine, moutarde de Meaux and soy sauce. Cook for a further 2 minutes. Add the cauliflower and chickpeas. Stir and cook for a further 1-2 minutes, then pour into the pie dish. Fit the pastry lid over the pie and glaze with the beaten egg, and bake for 45 minutes.

16

SPRING·MENU 5

PRAWN FILO PIE

•

ASPARAGUS TIMBALES

Filo pastry can now be bought more easily from shops. It is sometimes spelled phyllo, and is also sold as strudel pastry. If it is frozen, thaw overnight. What is not used can be kept in the refrigerator for a short period but this recipe needs 1 lb (450 g) of filo which is usually one packet.

Most recipes for filo pastry tell you to butter every sheet. This will give you an extremely rich pie, very high in saturated fats. In this recipe, I have suggested that you butter every second or third sheet. A balance must somehow be sought; if the pastry has not got enough fat, it will be very dry and unpleasant. If you are on a low-fat diet or must eschew all saturated fats, then the pie can be made substituting a polyunsaturated oil like sunflower or safflower instead of the butter.

Some people may think it an extravagance to purée asparagus, but it is one way of making a pound of this delectable vegetable serve six. Also the flavour of these timbales is very intense. For this recipe you could use sprue – the thin, feathery asparagus found at the end of the season – but then use 1½ lbs (675 g).

If you are feeling extravagant, garnish the pie with a few more prawns dusted with a little paprika. You could use a grapefruit and pistachio salad to end the meal, but any combination of fruit in season with a leaf would be satisfying to the palate.

PRAWN FILO PIE

Illustrated on page 18/19

— SERVES 6 —
---

1 lb (450 g) filo pastry sheets
20 Mediterranean prawns, cooked in the shell, or 2½ lb (1.1 kg) smaller prawns
12 oz (340 g) ricotta cheese
8 oz (225 g) feta, crumbled
2 large onions, minced
2 tablespoons celery seeds
2 teaspoons celery salt
1 tablespoon toasted sesame seeds
sea salt and freshly ground black pepper
a generous handful of parsley, chopped
butter for greasing
for the glaze
melted butter
poppy seeds

Peel the prawns. If using Mediterranean prawns, halve them lengthways; if using smaller prawns, leave them whole.

Mix together all the other ingredients, except the butter and poppy seeds.

Heat the oven to 400°F (200°C, gas mark 6).

Unfold the filo and cut the leaves in half with scissors, so that they are 9×12 in (23×30.5 cm). Butter a baking tray and lay 7-8 of the leaves on the tray, buttering every second or third one before the next two or three leaves are placed in position.

Spread one quarter of the cheese mixture over the filo and place another 7-8 leaves over it, brushing with butter as before. Spread one-third of the remaining cheese mixture over the filo and distribute the prawns over the surface. Spoon half the remaining cheese mixture over the prawns, then cover with 2 leaves of filo. Brush with butter and continue with the other sheets, spreading the filo with the remaining cheese mixture before the last 8 leaves are placed in position.

Brush the top of the pie with butter, sprinkle with >

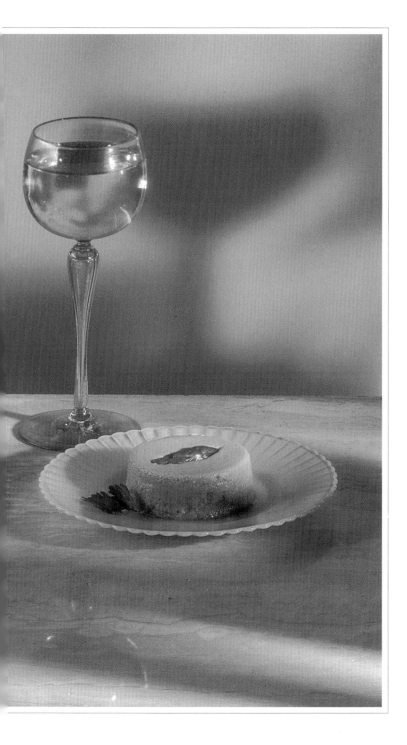

<poppy seeds and bake in the oven for 35-40 minutes, until golden brown. Remove from the oven and leave to stand for a few minutes before transferring to a heated serving dish. Serve cut into wedges.

ASPARAGUS TIMBALES

SERVES 6

1 lb (450 g) asparagus, trimmed
2 eggs, beaten
½ pint (280 ml) milk
sea salt and freshly ground black pepper

Cut off 6 of the asparagus tips and reserve. Simmer the remaining asparagus in a little boiling salted water, until tender.

Meanwhile, heat the oven to 400°F (200°C, gas mark 6).

Drain the asparagus well and blend to a purée in a blender or food processor. Add the eggs and milk and blend again. Season to taste with salt and pepper.

Butter 6 ramekins and place an asparagus tip in the bottom of each one. Pour in the asparagus mixture and bake in a bain marie for 20 minutes, or until set.

Remove from the oven and leave to stand for a few minutes before unmoulding.

Left; Prawn Filo Pie (page 17), right: Asparagus Timbale.

SPRING·MENU 6

MARINATED FISH SALAD

•

SLICED STUFFED AVOCADO

•

CELERY HERB ROLLS

This menu is for an al fresco luncheon in the sun, on one of those blissful spring days which seem like high summer. The lunch is an assembly job, arranging foods with a variety of flavours to satisfy the eye as well as the palate.

I have specified farmed salmon, because though it seems to me much inferior to wild salmon – having quite often a subcutaneous layer of fat which can even be unpleasant – it is a perfect fish for the marinade treatment. This, in fact, cold cooks it, completely transforming an inferior fish into a gourmet dish. The salmon can happily be left in the marinade for 2-3 days, if kept in the refrigerator.

Eat the meal with the freshly baked bread which is now much easier to make, since sachets of micronized yeast do not have to be fermented separately beforehand and the bread only has to rise once before it is baked. Various herbs can be added to the dough, but celery is one of my favourites.

MARINATED FISH SALAD

—— SERVES 6 ——

3 Finnan haddock
3 cutlets fresh farmed salmon (about 1 lb (450 g))
1 pint (560 ml) brown shrimps
1 pint (560 ml) peeled prawns
1 red pepper
1 green pepper
for the marinade
finely grated zest and juice of 1 lemon
¼ pint (150 ml) dry white wine
¼ pint (150 ml) fresh orange juice
finely grated zest of 2 oranges
3 tablespoons white wine vinegar
1 teaspoon Tabasco
1 tablespoon salt
1 tablespoon sugar

2-3 days in advance, make the marinade by mixing all the ingredients together. Then skin and bone the haddock and salmon cutlets and slice the flesh thinly. Place in the marinade and leave for 2-3 days.

Slice the tops from the peppers, core and seed them, then slice them into thin rings. Arrange the sliced peppers on a serving platter.

Drain the marinated fish and arrange in and over the peppers. Place the brown shrimps around the fish and make a border of the prawns round the edge of the platter.

Clockwise, from left: Marinated Fish Salad; Sliced Stuffed Avocado (page 22); Celery Herb Rolls (page 22).

SLICED STUFFED AVOCADO

Illustrated on page 21

——— SERVES 6 ———

2 large ripe avocados
5 oz (140 g) curd cheese
3 oz (85 g) feta cheese
1 bunch of spring onions, finely sliced
sea salt and freshly ground black pepper
juice of 1 lemon
for the garnish
lettuce leaves

Mix the two cheeses together with the spring onions and salt and pepper to taste. Cut the avocados in half and remove the stones, but do not peel them. Fill the cavities with the stuffing and then spread some on each of the two halves. Sandwich the avocados together again and chill in the refrigerator for 1 hour.

Arrange the lettuce leaves on a serving platter. Just before serving, cut the unpeeled avocados crossways into ½-in (1-cm) slices. Arrange over the lettuce leaves and paint the surface of the avocado with the lemon juice, using a pastry brush.

CELERY HERB ROLLS

Illustrated on page 21

——— MAKES 12 ROLLS OR 1 2-lb (900-kg) LOAF ———

1 lb (450 g) strong white unbleached flour
1 sachet easy-blend yeast
2 tablespoons celery seeds
2 teaspoons celery salt
1 teaspoon dill weed
pinch of sea salt
2 tablespoons olive oil
butter for greasing
poppy seeds, to decorate

Mix all the dry ingredients except the poppyseeds together thoroughly in a mixing bowl, then add the oil and ½ pint (280 ml) lukewarm water. Knead for 10 minutes by hand (or 5 minutes if using dough hooks and an electric mixer, if possible, as it takes the chore out of the task). Then form into 12 small rolls, or transfer to a well-buttered 2-lb (900-g) loaf tin. Leave to prove in a warm place for 1 hour.

Heat the oven to 425°F (220°C, gas mark 7).

Sprinkle the poppy seeds over the top of the rolls or loaf and bake the rolls for 15 minutes or the loaf for 40 minutes. When the tops are golden brown, remove a roll (or turn the bread out) from the oven and knock on its base; if it sounds hollow, it is cooked through. If not, bake in the oven for a further 5 minutes. Turn out on to a wire rack to cool.

SUMMER

The range of summer salads and herbs is so enormous that they can look as delightful as they taste. Think of leaves in varying shades: mix bronze, red and dappled lettuces, and toss golden with dark green leaves, deepening the tones with strips of black capsicum or dark plum. If you are making a simple tomato, pepper or courgette salad, choose varieties of different colours. A salad of red, green, yellow and black peppers spread over a bed of red, green, black and white beans looks quite splendid.

SUMMER·MENU 1

SEVICHE

•

MIXED GRAIN PILAF

People often confuse seviche or ceviche with caveach or escabeche. These are two separate recipes and methods of cooking, both ancient in history and both associated now with the New World, though they were introduced there by the Spaniards. The first, the seviche – spelt sometimes with a 'c' – is where the fish is cold-cooked in the marinade by the action of ascorbic acid – in this case, lime juice. The second recipe, for caveach or escabeche, requires the fish to be first fried and then pickled in a marinade of vinegar. (The word caveach *came via the Spanish from the Arab,* sakbay, *meaning meat or fish pickled in vinegar.)*

Both recipes were known in Roman times but I suspect they stem from the cuisine of the East. How interesting it is to note how dishes migrate, for these two methods of cooking and preserving fresh fish we now associate with Africa, Mexico, the West Indies and South America. All of these are hot countries, so the dishes are particularly enticing for the summer months.

Seviche is traditionally served on a large platter with slices of tomato, peppers, baby sweetcorn and hard-boiled egg. Since I believe that very often tradition knows best, I would keep roughly to this choice but arranged in a different pattern. If you serve the fish in the bowl in which it has marinated, you may get too much lime juice on your own plate. So serve it on a platter with just a garnish of coriander. Pile the pilaf in a bowl and in another, if you wish, contrive a salad of finely chopped peppers – red, green and yellow – mixed with sliced tomatoes and fresh baby sweetcorns (which have been lightly steamed or boiled), and cover with chopped hard-boiled egg, as in a mimosa salad. Toss the mixture in a light oil and white wine dressing. The sharp, clean seviche should dominate the meal.

SEVICHE

The selection of fish must be as fresh as possible. Try to use denser textured fish, such as those suggested below, although soft white fish like cod and haddock can be used, though they tend to disintegrate a bit and neither look as good or are quite chewy enough. But if you have to use them, slice the pieces slightly larger than for the fish used here.

--- **SERVES 6** ---

2½ lb (1100 g) mixture of fresh, dense, white fish, (angler or lotte, halibut, rockfish, scallops, John Dory, turbot, sea bass, swordfish or any of the shark family)
sea salt and freshly ground black pepper
juice and zest from about 5 limes
3 dried red chillies, broken up
4-5 cloves garlic, finely chopped
1 Spanish onion, red if available, finely sliced
1 bunch coriander leaves, finely chopped

Skin and bone all the fish, then cut into ½-in (1-cm) dice. Season the fish with salt and pepper and place in a large bowl. Take the zest from the limes and sprinkle it over the fish, then cover with the lime juice. Add the chillies, garlic and onion and give the mixture a good stir. Leave for half a day. Then, before serving, sprinkle over the coriander leaves.

Top: Mixed Grain Pilaf (page 26), below: Seviche.

MIXED GRAIN PILAF
Illustrated on page 24/25

———————— SERVES 6 ————————

3 oz (85 g) couscous
3 oz (85 g) buckwheat
3 oz (85 g) millet
2 onions
½ lb (225 g) fresh garden peas
a handful of mint, finely chopped
sea salt and freshly ground black pepper

Pour water over the couscous, then drain immediately. Let the grains stand for 15 minutes; then crumble them in your fingers to break up the lumps.

Meanwhile, in a little salted water, boil the buckwheat for 10 minutes and, when tender, drain.

Then simmer the millet, covered, for 20 minutes. Place the couscous over the millet in a steamer or colander and steam at the same time. Cook the peas by boiling in a little salted water for 5-8 minutes. Drain the peas and reserve.

Remove the steamed couscous from over the millet. Drain the millet and combine all the grains in a large bowl together with the onions.

Add the reserved peas and the mint. Season to taste.

SUMMER · MENU 2

VINE LEAF PARCELS OF FISH

•

BROAD BEAN PUREE

•

COURGETTES TEMPURA

Vine leaves can be bought in packets, pickled in brine. To prepare for use, pour boiling water over and allow them to float free, then rinse them in cold water to remove the salt. Or if you are lucky enough to have a vine, you can use your own vine leaves. Pick them in spring and early summer only, since by autumn they are too tough. If you are using fresh leaves, blanch them for a few minutes.

The flavour of the vine permeates the fish and gives it a slightly smoky flavour. It blends well with the Broad Bean Purée, which should be tempered with a pinch of summer savory. Take care, though, as the herb is strong and can swamp a dish.

Let the parcels of wrapped fish stand for a few hours before cooking to develop the flavour. The Courgettes Tempura should be cooked immediately before serving, but both the bean purée and the fish parcels can be allowed to rest while the tempura is being prepared.

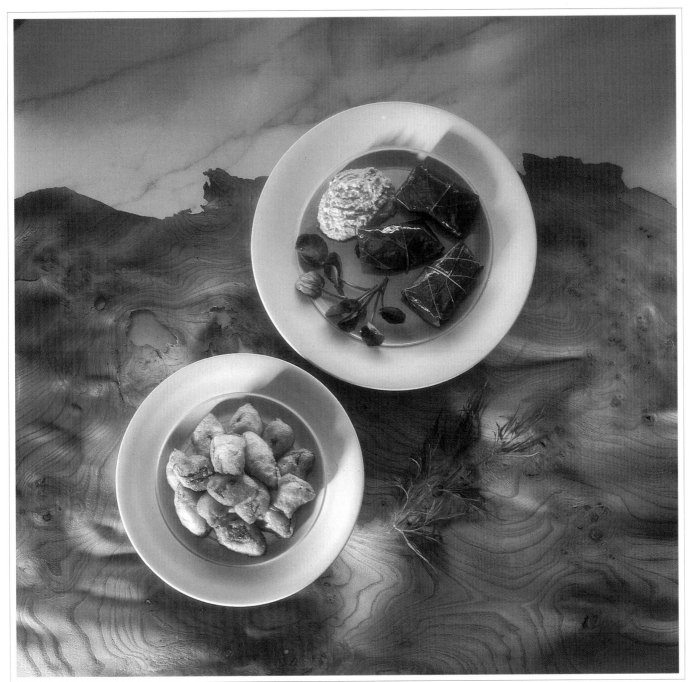

Below: Courgettes Tempura (page 28), top: Broad Bean Purée (page 28), Vine Leaf Parcels of Fish (page 28).

VINE LEAF PARCELS OF FISH
Illustrated on page 27

——————— SERVES 6 ———————

4-6 cutlets of cod, hake, huss, dogfish or haddock
8-12 vine leaves
sea salt and freshly ground black pepper
2 tablespoons fresh dill weed
2 oz (50 g) butter
¼ pint (150 ml) dry white wine
zest and juice of 1 lemon
for the garnish
sprigs of watercress

If using fresh vine leaves, blanch them in boiling water for 2 minutes, then drain. If using canned, pour over boiling water, gently separate, then drain and rinse in cold water. Pat the leaves dry before using.

Divide the cutlets in half or, if they are large, into three, ensuring that the vine leaves will enclose the fish completely. Lay a portion of fish on each vine leaf. Sprinkle with the sea salt, pepper, a little dill weed and a knob of butter. Fold the ends of the leaf into the centre and wrap the fish completely.

Lay the parcels in a flameproof-dish and wedge the pieces in against each other to ensure they stay closed during cooking. Pour over the wine, lemon juice and zest and bring to simmering point. Lower the heat and cook for 12 minutes. Turn off the heat and let the fish parcels settle for 5 minutes before arranging on a heated platter. Garnish with the watercress.

BROAD BEAN PUREE
Illustrated on page 27

——————— SERVES 6 ———————

2 lb (900 g) young broad beans
sea salt and freshly ground black pepper
a pinch of fresh summer savory or thyme
¼ pint (150 ml) Greek yoghurt

Try to use young beans, since they do not need their inner shell peeled. Pod the beans and boil in salted water for 8-10 minutes.

Put into a blender with a little sea salt, lots of freshly ground black pepper, the summer savory and the yoghurt. Blend to a thick purée. Reheat gently, top with a little butter and keep warm until served.

COURGETTES TEMPURA
Illustrated on page 27

——————— SERVES 6 ———————

1½ lb (675 g) courgettes
for the tempura
1 egg, separated
¼ lb (120 g) plain flour
¼ pint (150 ml) iced water
sea salt

Mix the egg yolk with the sifted flour. When well combined, pour in the water slowly, beating energetically.

Whip the egg white until it is stiff and fold it into the batter.

Slice the courgettes lengthways down the centre and then divide each half into three horizontally. Dip each piece of courgette into the batter and deep-fry in corn oil for about a minute, until the batter is golden and crisp.

SUMMER · MENU 3

TUNA FISH CASSEROLE

·

WILD RICE SALAD

Tuna is the one fish that can marry well with strong flavours. This recipe originates in the Mediterranean where variations occur from Turkey to Spain.

Raw tuna is a red and rather bloody fish. To non-meat eaters it may look a bit like steak. I have found that its flavour is much improved if it is washed beneath a cold tap, until the colour changes from dark red to beige.

Wild rice is not strictly a rice at all. It grows along the lake-shores of Minnesota and is picked by hand – still in some cases by American Indians – which is why it is expensive. It looks beautiful and has a singular and delicious flavour. It is also nutritionally far superior to any form of rice and, cooked, will yield three times the amount. You can, as I have done here, mix it successfully with brown rice to make a less extravagant dish.

TUNA FISH CASSEROLE

Illustrated on page 30/31

—— SERVES 6 ——

2½ lb (1100 g) tuna steaks
plain flour
3 fl oz (80 ml) olive oil
1 teaspoon dried oregano or marjoram
1 teaspoon dried thyme
1 teaspoon dried rosemary
2 onions, sliced
5 cloves garlic, sliced
2 red peppers, cored, seeded and sliced
sea salt and freshly ground black pepper
2 lb (900 g) tomatoes, peeled and chopped

Heat the oven to 350°F (180°C, gas mark 4).

Wash the fish, then pat it dry. Slice into large pieces and dip each piece in flour.

Heat the oil in a large flameproof casserole and add the herbs, onion and garlic. Drop the fish pieces in one by one and fry briefly on both sides, pushing pieces over to make room for the next. Add the peppers and fry them gently. Season well with the salt and pepper. Stir in the tomatoes and then place the casserole in the preheated oven and bake for 40 minutes.

WILD RICE SALAD

SERVES 6

4 oz (120 g) wild rice
4 oz (120 g) brown rice
2 oz (50 g) butter
zest of 1 lemon plus 1 tablespoon juice
1 lb (450 g) fresh peas from the pod
sea salt and freshly ground black pepper
handful of finely chopped parsley

Wash the wild rice under cold water in a colander and drain immediately. Place the rice in a saucepan and pour in enough boiling water to cover it; simmer for 5 minutes. Turn the heat off and let the rice stand for an hour or more to cook slowly and absorb the water. This phase can be done earlier in the day.

Boil the peas for 12 minutes or until they are tender. Bring the wild rice back to the boil and simmer for 20 minutes. Drain both the peas and the wild rice thoroughly.

Meanwhile, cover and simmer the brown rice, depending on the type you have chosen, for the time it takes to make it tender — anything from 20 to 45 minutes. Drain thoroughly. Combine the peas and the rice and add the lemon zest and juice, butter and chopped parsley. Toss the rice and season well. Serve warm or at room temperature.

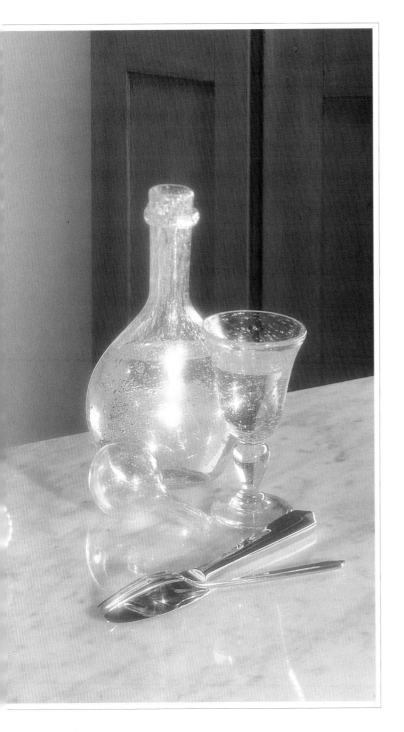

SUMMER·MENU 4

SMOKED SWORDFISH

•

POTATO AND PARSLEY CUSTARDS

•

TOMATOES PROVENÇALE

Buying a small hot smoker can be a worthwhile invest-ment. I have had one for over twenty years and, wherever I live, I invest in another if the old one has been mislaid or I've given it away.

A hot smoker is a kind of glorified mess tin. Sawdust goes in the bottom and is covered with a plate of tin. The slightly salted fish is placed on a small grill above that, and a tightly fitting lid goes on top. A fire is lit below the tin and the fish is hot smoked – actually cooked – within 12 minutes. An effortless form of cooking, it can transform dull or tasteless fish. Not that swordfish is either; but bought in England, it is bound to come frozen, and will lack much of its original flavour. Hot smoking is perfect for it. If it is unavailable, halibut has the dense texture which makes a suitable substitute.

There should be a good portion of parsley to balance the potato in the vegetable dish. It should be speckled a dark green and taste strongly of the herb. Serve topped with a little butter.

As to the tomatoes, this is the perfect Mediterranean dish to complement the fish, king of that landbound sea. Marmande tomatoes are the big tomatoes, im-ported from France and Morocco. They are more ex-pensive than our plain round, smooth little cousins, but their flavour is so much richer.

Top: Wild Rice Salad, below: Tuna Fish Casserole (page 29).

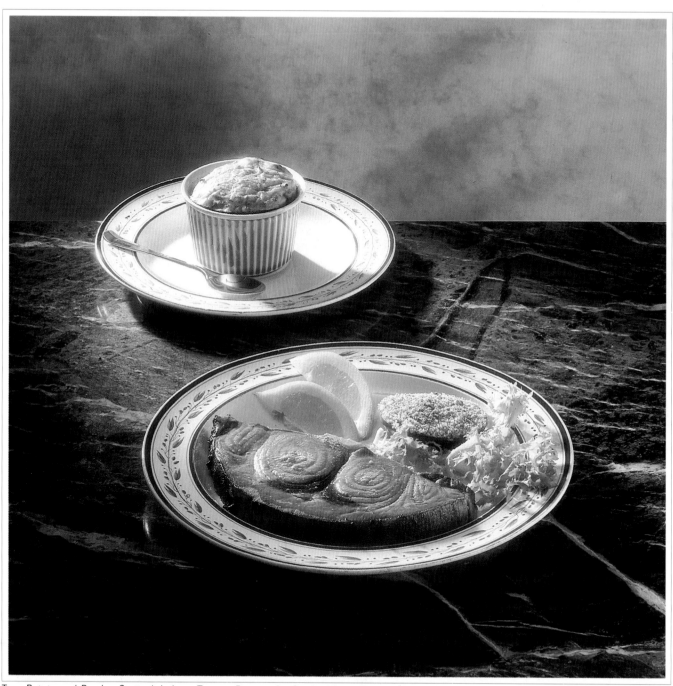

Top: Potato and Parsley Custard, below: Tomato Provençale, Smoked Swordfish.

SMOKED SWORDFISH

SERVES 6

4-6 swordfish steaks or halibut steaks
sea salt
for the garnish
lemons, quartered

Dust the steaks with salt and hot-smoke them for 12 minutes. Leave them in the smoker, unopened, for up to half an hour afterwards.

Serve warm with the quartered lemons.

POTATO AND PARSLEY CUSTARDS

SERVES 6
---

1 lb (450 g) potatoes, boiled and mashed
1 oz (25 g) butter
½ pint (280 ml) milk
1 teaspoon sea salt and freshly ground black pepper
2 eggs, beaten
4 tablespoons finely chopped parsley

Heat the oven to 400°F (200°C, gas mark 6).

Mix all the ingredients together into a smooth batter. Grease six ramekins well and fill them two-thirds full with the batter. Place in a bain marie and pour water into it so that it comes halfway up the sides of the ramekins. Bake for 20 minutes in the preheated oven until firm.

The custards can be served topped with Greek yoghurt which has been mixed with more chopped parsley.

TOMATOES PROVENÇALE

SERVES 6

4-6 large Marmande tomatoes (allow one for each person)
6-8 cloves garlic
1 teaspoon sea salt
dried breadcrumbs

Slice the tomatoes in half. Cut a grill pattern to a depth of about ¼ in (6 mm) into the sliced surface. Crush the garlic cloves thoroughly in a bowl and mix with the sea salt. Smear the garlic paste on the surface of the prepared tomatoes and sprinkle with the breadcrumbs. Place under a hot grill until the surface bubbles and blackens slightly.

Left: Cheese Brioche (page 37), centre: Avocado Mousse (page 36) and Courgettes Stuffed with Gooseberry Purée, right: Mixed Green and Red Bean Salad (page 37).

SUMMER · MENU 5

AVOCADO MOUSSE

•

COURGETTES STUFFED
WITH GOOSEBERRY PUREE

•

MIXED GREEN AND RED BEAN SALAD

•

CHEESE BRIOCHE

This is a summer menu, for lunch or dinner. It can be prepared the day before, with only the details to complete half an hour before you want to eat. What bliss such arrangements are; you can relax totally and enjoy your guests.

Make the mousse, the beans and the stuffed courgettes the day before. Leave the fun bits until last – garnishing the courgettes, adding the vegetables to the bean salad and unmoulding the mousse. The latter is light and must be sliced gently.

This is a meal which would benefit from a homemade bread or brioche, baked earlier that morning. Brioches are rich in butter and eggs, and thus high in saturated fats, but they are wonderfully delicious. Eaten only once or twice in the year, a treat in an otherwise balanced diet, they should do no harm.

I always use now the sachets of micronized yeast which do not require starting first. A sachet can be added dry to the rest of the ingredients and the dough only needs to prove once. I find a food processor fitted with dough hooks indispensable for bread-making, as I rarely have the patience to knead for 10 minutes. But in addition, because the brioche dough is extra sticky, the hooks are almost a practical necessity. If kneading by hand, flour the hands continually.

35

COURGETTES STUFFED WITH GOOSEBERRY PUREE

Illustrated on page 34/35

──────── SERVES 6 ────────

4-6 small courgettes
½ lb (225 g) gooseberries
5 oz (140 g) curd cheese
for the garnish
1 courgette

Trim and slice the courgettes in half lengthways. Cut out the seeds and enough of the flesh to leave a medium-thick shell, and discard them. Steam the shells for 10 minutes.

Meanwhile, place the gooseberries in a saucepan, without any water or sugar, over a very low heat; simmer until they are actually boiling. Give them a stir and take away from the heat. Mash them coarsely and let them cool. Then remove all extra juice from them by placing them in a colander or sieve and allowing them to drain.

Mix the curd cheese with the gooseberries thoroughly and stuff the courgette shells with the mixture. Grate the raw courgette and sprinkle a little over the stuffing.

AVOCADO MOUSSE

Illustrated on page 34/35

──────── SERVES 6 ────────

3 medium-size ripe avocadoes
½ pint (280 ml) smetana
zest of 1 lemon plus 2 tablespoons juice
¾ oz (20 g) gelatine
4 fl oz (110 ml) dry white wine
sea salt and freshly ground pepper
2 egg whites, beaten
a generous bunch of parsley
a generous bunch of mint
for the garnish
extra mint leaves or salad burnet

Peel and stone the avocadoes. Place the flesh in a blender or food processor, together with the smetana, lemon zest and juice. Process until it forms smooth paste. Melt the gelatine in the white wine and stir that into the avocado mixture. Season generously, using white pepper if you want the creamy flesh unspeckled.

In a medium-sized bowl, beat the egg whites until they are stiff and carefully fold them into the avocado mixture in the processor bowl. Finely chop the parsley and place it in one bowl, then finely chop the mint and place in another. Take some of the avocado mixture – about 4 heaped tablespoons – and mix it into the chopped parsley. Take another 4 tablespoons and mix into the chopped mint.

Moisten the interior of a 2½ pint (1400 ml) soufflé dish. Decorate the base with two or three salad burnet or mint leaves in an artistic pattern. Place some of the avocado mixture on the bottom and smooth it down. Cover with a layer of the parsley mixture, followed by another of the plain and then another of the mint mixture. Continue in layers until all mixtures are used up.

Place the soufflé dish in the refrigerator for a day to set. Unmould by briefly dipping the base of the dish into hot water then turning the mould over onto a platter.

MIXED GREEN
AND RED BEAN SALAD

Illustrated on page 34/35

———————— SERVES 6 ————————

5 oz (140 g) green flageolet beans
4 oz (120 g) red kidney beans
sea salt and freshly ground black pepper
2 dried red chillies
1 teaspoon green peppercorns
2 tablespoons olive oil
1 teaspoon white wine vinegar
zest and juice of 1 lemon
2 tablespoons walnut oil
6-8 young spinach leaves
1 bunch spring onions
2-3 baby carrots

Keep the beans separate throughout the cooking process.

Soak the flageolet and kidney beans overnight in separate bowls and cook them separately, adding to the kidney beans the 2 crumbled dried red chillies. When they are cooked (the kidney beans should take only 1½ hours; the flageolet about 1 hour), drain them thoroughly, then season with salt and pepper.

To the flageolet beans, add the green peppercorns, the olive oil and the wine vinegar. To the red kidney beans, add the zest and juice of the lemon and the walnut oil. Let both the beans stand, covered, for at least half a day.

Before serving, chop up the spinach leaves very finely with the spring onions. Mix them with the flageolet beans. Grate the carrots and stir them into the red kidney beans. Choose a large platter and arrange some of the red beans in the centre, then encircle them with the green flageolet. Finish with an outer border of the kidney beans.

CHEESE BRIOCHE

Illustrated on page 34/35

———————— SERVES 6 ————————

10 oz (275 g) strong white bread flour
4 oz (120 g) butter, grated
4 oz (120 g) mature farmhouse Cheddar cheese, grated
1 teaspoon salt
3 eggs, beaten
1 sachet yeast

Heat the oven to 375°F (190°C, gas mark 5)

Sieve the flour. Take the butter straight from the refrigerator and grate it and the cheese into the flour. Mix thoroughly. Add the rest of the ingredients and begin to knead – with dough hooks, if available. Knead the dough for 5-6 minutes, then place it in a brioche tin or, if unavailable, a bread tin. Cover and leave in a warm place to rise for about half an hour.

Bake the brioche in the preheated oven for 20-25 minutes. Turn out on to a wire rack to cool.

SUMMER · MENU 6

ASPARAGUS CLAMART

·

LENTIL KEFTETHES

·

COLCANNON

How good globe artichokes are and, when they are first in season, what luxury to use great numbers of these baby ones. They have not grown large enough to have that spiky choke in the centre or the pad of flesh, the artichoke bottom used in the casserole on page 58. Their flavour is fresh and intense. Mixed with asparagus and garden peas, this dish seems to me to be sybaritic bliss. It is called 'Clamart', named after a district in Paris where peas used to be grown. Any combination now of peas with other summer vegetables is named after it.

I have teamed it with a famous Irish dish, Colcannon, to help soak up the clamart sauce. But Colcannon itself is not known or enjoyed enough outside Ireland. And lastly, I have chosen a little Greek ball which, in its spiciness, stems further east of the Mediterranean and must come from Persia or the shores of India. This is to ensure that your palate is not lulled to sleep by the quiet subtlety of the other dishes. Asafoetida – a favourite herb of mine – grows in the Middle East and resembles a large fennel root. I would pile these lentil balls up into a pyramid shape and serve them on a platter or plate, dusted perhaps with a little paprika. While the Colcannon is served in a bowl, the clamart in its sauce should also be on a platter so that its range of summer vegetables is shown in all its enticing harmony.

ASPARAGUS CLAMART

──────── SERVES 6 ────────

4-6 small fresh globe artichokes
peel and juice of 1 lemon
1 lb (450 g) asparagus
1 lb (450 g) fresh garden peas, shelled
2 oz (50 g) butter
1 young cos lettuce
1 tablespoon double cream
sea salt and freshly ground black pepper

Discard the outer leaves of the artichokes and quarter each one. Add the lemon peel and juice, a little salt and the artichoke hearts to 1 pint (560 ml) of water in a saucepan. Simmer for 10 minutes, then take the artichoke hearts out of the water with a slotted spoon and drain well, reserving the water.

In the same water, simmer the trimmed asparagus spears for 6 minutes. Remove them from the water, keeping it, and drain the spears well. Now simmer the shelled peas in the same water for 10 minutes or until tender. Take from the water with the slotted spoon, and allow them to drain. Reduce the water to about 1/4 pint (150 ml). Discard the lemon peel.

Melt the butter in a shallow flameproof gratin dish. Separate the leaves of the lettuce, discarding the outer damaged ones. Cook the inner lettuce leaves in the butter for a few minutes, then add the peas, the reduced stock and the artichokes. Simmer for a minute or two, then add the asparagus, cream and seasoning. Stir to combine, then place under a hot grill until the sauce is bubbling.

Top: Colcannon (page 40), centre: Lentil Keftethes (page 40), below: Asparagus Clamart.

LENTIL KEFTETHES
Illustrated on page 39

––––––––––– SERVES 6 –––––––––––

4 oz (120 g) green or brown lentils
2 tablespoons olive oil
½ teaspoon each crushed cumin and cardomom
1 teaspoon each turmeric and asafoetida
1 tablespoon gram (besan) flour
sea salt and freshly ground black pepper
toasted breadcrumbs
corn oil for frying

Soak the lentils for one hour, then drain them. Heat the olive oil in a large frying pan, add the cumin and cardomom, followed by the lentils. Cover with water and simmer gently for 40 minutes, or until soft. Drain the lentils thoroughly and place in a blender with the turmeric, asafoetida, seasoning and flour. Blend to a thick purée. Refrigerate for about 1 hour. Then roll into balls in your hands, and coat with the breadcrumbs. Heat the corn oil in a large frying pan, and fry the balls in the hot oil. Remove one by one with a slotted spoon and keep warm in a low oven at 225°F (110°C, gas mark ¼) until ready to serve.

COLCANNON
Illustrated on page 39

––––––––––– SERVES 6 –––––––––––

½ lb (225 g) kale, spring greens, chard or cabbage
1 bunch spring onions
¼ pint (150 ml) milk
2 oz (50 g) butter
2 lb (900 g) floury potatoes, peeled
sea salt and freshly ground black pepper

Remove and discard the fibrous stems from the greens and slice the leaves very, very thinly. They should be razor thin. Place them in a saucepan with a very little boiling salted water, cook fiercely for 2 minutes, and then drain. Slice the spring onions very finely, put in the same saucepan, together with the milk and butter, and simmer for 3 minutes.

Boil the potatoes in a large saucepan until tender, then drain thoroughly. Return them to the saucepan, mash them until smooth, season to taste, add the greens, and then the milk and onion mixture. Beat vigorously so that the Colcannon is light and airy. Heap on to a serving dish and add an extra knob of butter in the centre.

AUTUMN

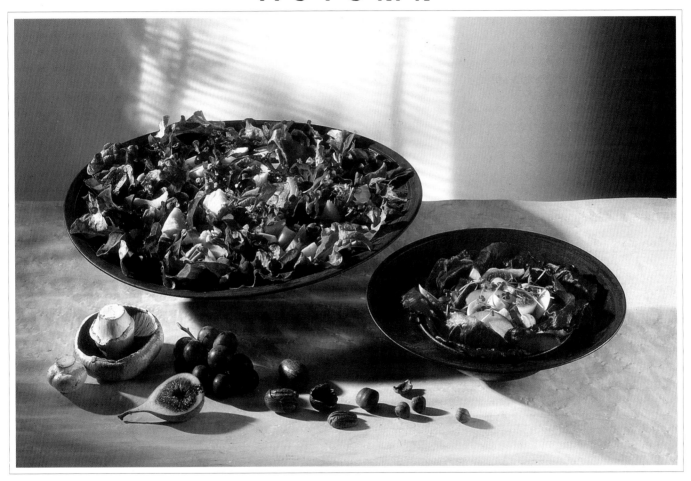

Certain very good salad vegetables appear only in the autumn.
The delicious red and green variegated lettuces, chicories and
endives – like radicchio – appear now, their colour turning as
the climate gets colder. Their slight bitterness can be balanced
by adding a fruit, like soaked dried apricots, to the ingredients.
Mushrooms and funghi also appear. Field mushrooms are
excellent raw, combined with a little chopped onion, in an oil
and lemon dressing. Perhaps the most remarkable autumn
salad is globe artichokes, if you can find them at the right
price.

AUTUMN · MENU 1

FILLETS OF WHITE FISH STUFFED WITH MUSHROOMS

·

BULGAR WHEAT AND MINT PILAF

·

BAKED RED PEPPERS IN TOMATO SAUCE

Fillets of flat fish are easily rolled around a stuffing and then lightly poached. Any member of the sole family provides perfect fillets. Dover sole has, of course, the best flavour.

White wine sauce can usually be counted on to reduce during cooking but, as I want to poach the fish in the wine and then use the cooking liquor to make the sauce, the time required to cook the fish is not enough to reduce the cooking liquor. So I have left the sauce a bit on the thin side, but its delicate grapey, creamy flavour goes excellently with this well-flavoured fish and its mushroom stuffing.

All fish dishes must be cooked just before serving, but the fish can be prepared and stuffed some hours before. The baked red peppers and tomatoes need long, slow cooking, so these can be put on hours before. Soak the bulgar wheat earlier, then heat it in the oven in the last 20 minutes, while the peppers are cooking. Stir in the chopped mint at the last moment.

Serve the pilaf and the peppers as side dishes, or, depending on whim, treat the two dishes as a course on their own, after the fish. But they do go well with the fish and provide an excellent and nutritious contrast – for both the palate and the eye.

FILLETS OF WHITE FISH STUFFED WITH MUSHROOMS

———— SERVES 6 ————

12 fillets of white fish
½ pint (280 ml) dry white wine
sea salt and freshly ground black pepper
for the mushroom stuffing
½ lb (225 g) mushrooms
1 oz (25 g) butter
1 teaspoon freshly chopped coriander
1 oz (25 g) breadcrumbs
3 oz (85 g) curd or ricotta cheese
sea salt and freshly ground black pepper
for the white wine sauce
3-4 shallots
1 oz (25 g) butter
1 tablespoon thick cream

First make the stuffing. Slice the mushrooms thinly. Melt the butter in a medium-size saucepan, add the coriander and the mushrooms. Cook them over a low to medium heat until soft. Leave them to cool, then place in a blender or food processor and process with the breadcrumbs, cheese, salt and pepper to a chunky purée. Place in a mixing bowl and refrigerate for an hour.

Now make the sauce. Slice the shallots thinly. Melt the butter in a saucepan and cook the shallots on high for a few minutes, until they are soft. Take from the heat and reserve.

Spoon a tablespoon of stuffing on to the end of a fillet. Roll up the fillet carefully and secure with a tooth pick. Lay the rolled fillets carefully one by one in a thick-bottomed flameproof casserole which has a lid. Pour the wine over, then season with salt and pepper. Bring the liquid to simmering point. Place the lid on the casserole and continue to simmer for 4-5 minutes. Remove the fillets gently from the casserole, place on >

Top: Fillets of White Fish Stuffed with Mushrooms, with Bulgar Wheat and Mint Pilaf (page 44), below: Baked Red Peppers in Tomato Sauce (page 44).

< a serving dish and keep them warm.

Pour the liquid from the fish into the saucepan containing the butter and shallots. Boil fiercely for a few minutes so that the sauce reduces by a third. Take the saucepan off the heat and stir in the cream. Pour the sauce over the fish and serve.

BULGAR WHEAT AND MINT PILAF

Illustrated on page 43

―――――――――― SERVES 6 ――――――――――

1 bunch spring onions
2 generous handfuls of mint leaves
6 oz (170 g) bulgar wheat
zest and juice of 2 lemons
sea salt and freshly ground black pepper

Chop the onions finely and one of the handfuls of mint. Mix these thoroughly with the bulgar wheat. Add the zest and juice from the 2 lemons. Pour over boiling water to cover and leave for a few hours.

Twenty minutes before the pilaf is to be served, place in an ovenproof dish, cover with a lid, and put it in the oven at the same temperature as the baked peppers.

When the pilaf is ready, remove it from the oven. Chop the second handful of mint finely and stir it into the pilaf with salt and pepper to taste.

BAKED RED PEPPERS IN TOMATO SAUCE

Illustrated on page 43

―――――――――― SERVES 6 ――――――――――

4-5 red peppers, cored, seeded, sliced in wide strips
10 cloves garlic
3 fl oz (75 ml) olive oil
1½ lb (675 g) tomatoes, peeled and chopped
1 tablespoon marjoram, chopped
sea salt and freshly ground black pepper

Heat the oven to 325°F (160°C, gas mark 3).

Heat the olive oil in an oven- and flameproof dish, and add the peppers, garlic and marjoram. Cook for a moment, then stir in the tomatoes, salt and pepper. Bake in the oven for 3 hours.

AUTUMN · MENU 2

SPICED PRAWNS BARBECUED
WITH SATAY SAUCE

•

MILLET CASSEROLE
WITH PISTACHIO NUTS

•

GRATIN OF PUMPKIN WITH GINGER

This is an early autumnal meal to be enjoyed outside. I have suggested a barbecue because there is a special, almost primeval, satisfaction about cooking over an open fire outdoors. Yet no one could pretend that barbecuing refines food when cooking it; quite the opposite. But in the following spiced prawn recipe, the shells protect the flesh inside. At the same time, by opening the shells up beforehand, you allow the marinade to do its work.

The accompanying dishes in this meal are best eaten lukewarm to cool, so they are suitable for an outside barbecue. Never be afraid of eating pieces of ginger itself. Sliced thinly enough and coated with honey and pumpkin, as they are here, they are delicious. Both the gratin and the millet casserole can be made earlier in the day and then briefly reheated. Both dishes, I believe, benefit from this treatment.

SPICED PRAWNS BARBECUED WITH SATAY SAUCE

Illustrated on page 46/47

———————— SERVES 6 ————————

20-30 large Mediterranean prawns, cooked
for the marinade
¼ pint (150 ml) red wine vinegar
1 tablespoon honey
2 oz (50 g) grated ginger root
1 tablespoon salt
1 teaspoon cayenne pepper
zest and juice of 2 lemons
1 tablespoon brandy
for the sauce
3 cloves garlic, crushed
2 dried red chillies, crushed
3 tablespoons shoyu (Japanese soya) sauce
1 tablespoon brown sugar
½ teaspoon salt
4 oz (120 g) peanut butter
2 oz (50 g) dried coconut

To make the marinade, heat the red wine vinegar. Melt the honey in it, and add the grated ginger root, salt and cayenne pepper. Stir in the zest and juice from the lemons, followed by the brandy.

Slice the shell of each prawn, from the bottom of the head to the tail, to expose the flesh; but keep the head and shell on. Place the prawns in a shallow dish and pour the marinade over. Leave for a day.

To make the sauce, mix the first six ingredients together and set aside. Grate the dried coconut into a saucepan, add enough water to cover it by an inch and gently heat, until the coconut forms a smooth sauce. Stir in the rest of the ingredients, and heat gently.

To barbecue, ensure the charcoal is covered in grey ash. That is when the heat is at its best. Allow about five prawns to each skewer. Cook until the shells are just edged with brown – about 4-5 minutes.

45

Left: Millet Casserole with Pistachio Nuts, centre: Spiced Prawns Barbecued with Satay Sauce (page 45), right: Gratin of Pumpkin with Ginger.

MILLET CASSEROLE WITH PISTACHIO NUTS

---------------- SERVES 6 ----------------

3 oz (85 g) pistachio nuts, shelled and peeled
1½ oz (40 g) butter
2 cloves garlic, crushed
4 oz (120 g) millet
½ pint (280 ml) fish stock
sea salt and freshly ground black pepper
3 fl oz (75 ml) dry vermouth

Roughly grind 2 oz (50 g) of the pistachio nuts, reserving the remainder. Melt 1 oz (25 g) of the butter in a thick-bottomed flameproof oven dish, stir in the garlic and millet, then add the fish stock and the nuts. Bring the mixture to the boil, then simmer for 20 minutes. Season to taste. Stir in the reserved whole pistachio nuts, dry vermouth and the remainder of the butter.

GRATIN OF PUMPKIN WITH GINGER

---------------- SERVES 6 ----------------

3 tablespoons olive oil
12 oz (340 g) pumpkin flesh, cubed
3 oz (85 g) ginger root, peeled and thinly sliced
2 tablespoons honey
sea salt and freshly ground black pepper
1 tablespoon toasted sesame seeds

Heat the oil in a frying pan and add the pumpkin and ginger. Fry quite fiercely, moving the vegetables around the pan. Cook for about 5-6 minutes. When the pumpkin pieces are crisp-soft, season, pour over the honey, and sprinkle on the sesame seeds. Place the pan under a hot grill until the honey bubbles and reduces.

47

AUTUMN · MENU 3

ROAST PHEASANT
WITH BLACKCURRANT SAUCE

·

GRATIN JURASSIENNE

·

BRAISED CELERY

Many people think of the pheasant as a dry bird, which is why it is so often casseroled. But pheasants can be successfully roasted if well-coated in butter or covered in bacon fat, or cooked breast-side down. But these solutions create their own irony: a bird without saturated fats in its flesh has them added in the cooking. An obvious absurdity.

The following method roasts 2-3 pheasants with a little wine and so keeps them moist. Using a sealed roasting bag also prevents the birds from drying out. Pheasant goes well with sharp fruits, and blackcurrants possess the most distinctive flavour of all the berries. The seasons for both do not quite overlap, but currants freeze well.

This subtle combination seems to cry out for a classic potato gratin, with crisp medallions of golden spud on the top hiding the soft, creamy inside. I have used another berry here – the juniper – because its clean, astringent flavour links the bird with the vegetables. The celery is very simply braised, complementing the game beautifully.

These three dishes are all cooked in the oven at 350°F (180°C, gas mark 4). Begin with the gratin, 2½ hours before serving. After 1½ hours, place the gratin at the very bottom of the oven and raise the heat to 400°F (200°C, gas mark 6). Place the pheasants on the top rack to cook. The celery can go in at the same time, but in the lower part of the oven, just above the gratin. If this proves too difficult, the celery can be lightly poached on top of the stove.

48

ROAST PHEASANT
WITH BLACKCURRANT SAUCE

——— SERVES 6 ———

2 rosemary twigs
2-3 hen pheasants (allow 1 for 2 people)
1 onion, sliced
5 cloves garlic, crushed
½ pint (280 ml) red wine
sea salt and freshly ground black pepper
1 lb (450 g) blackcurrants, fresh or frozen
for the garnish
lemon balm or mint

Heat the oven to 400°F (200°C, gas mark 6).

Break up the rosemary twigs and stuff the birds with them. Then place the birds inside a large roasting bag, scatter the onion and garlic around them and pour in the wine. Season with salt and pepper, and tie up the bag – but do *not* perforate it.

Place the bag in a large baking dish and put into the top of the oven for 1 hour. Meanwhile, place the blackcurrants in a small, heavy saucepan and bring them to the boil. Turn off the heat and drain most of the juice away from the currants into a small bowl. Open the bag containing the pheasants. Drain all the liquid and the now softened onion and garlic into a blender. Add the currant juice and blend to a purée. Heat in a saucepan and reduce by half, then combine this sauce with the blackcurrants themselves.

Slice the pheasants in two and discard the rosemary. Cut off the legs and wings to serve separately. Then peel off the skin from the breasts and slice the flesh quite thickly. Pour the currant sauce over a platter and arrange the breast slices on top of it. Garnish with a small amount of fresh lemon balm or mint.

Above: Roast Pheasant with Blackcurrant Sauce, Gratin Jurassiene (page 50), Braised Celery (page 50).

GRATIN JURASSIENNE
Illustrated on page 49

—— SERVES 6 ——

2 lb (900 g) potatoes, peeled and thinly sliced
¼ pint (150 ml) skimmed milk
½ pint (280 ml) smetana
3 oz (85 g) Gruyère cheese, thinly sliced
1 oz (25 g) juniper berries, roughly crushed
a pinch of nutmeg
sea salt and freshly ground black pepper

Heat the oven to 350°F (180°C, gas mark 4).

Soak the sliced potatoes in cold water for ½ an hour, then rinse them under cold water. Pat the slices dry.

Beat the milk into the smetana. Butter a large shallow oven dish and line the base with potato. Scatter the Gruyère slices over, and follow with a sprinkling of juniper berries, nutmeg, salt and pepper. Pour over a small amount of the smetana and milk mixture. Continue layering until finished. Bake for 2½ hours, until the potatoes are tender and the dish is creamy.

BRAISED CELERY
Illustrated on page 49

—— SERVES 6 ——

3 heads of celery, cleaned of outer stalks
1 oz (25 g) butter
¼ pint (150 ml) vermouth or dry white wine
sea salt and freshly ground black pepper

Trim the root and slice each celery heart in two. Melt the butter in a large flameproof dish and lay the 6 celery halves in it. Pour over the vermouth and season to taste. Bake with the gratin, but for only 1 hour.

AUTUMN · MENU 4

WALNUT AND BRUSSELS SPROUT TIMBALE WITH TOMATO SAUCE

•

LEEK, POTATO AND OLIVE GRATIN

•

GLAZED BEETROOT

With what relief sometimes do we view a complete meal of vegetables, with all their freshness and appeal, untainted by little corpses. This meal for autumn includes two classic combinations of flavours; walnuts with Brussels sprouts and cabbage is one. Formed into a timbale, it is unmoulded and then cut like a cake. The glossy, crinkly green exterior is set off with a tomato sauce, good to look at and delicious in flavour. There are also glazed baby beetroots.

Leek and potatoes is the other classic combination, but here they are cooked in wine and given a bit of pep (I cannot abide boring food) by the slivers of black olive.

The timbale and its sauce can be prepared some hours earlier in the day. The beetroots can be cooked before too, then glazed at the last minute. Even the gratin will not be harmed in the least by being cooked ahead up to the point just before the addition of the olives.

Clockwise, from left: Walnut and Brussels Sprout Timbale (page 52), Leek, Potato and Olive Gratin (page 52), Glazed Beetroot (page 52).

WALNUT AND BRUSSELS SPROUT TIMBALE

Illustrated on page 51

─────── SERVES 6 ───────

4 large Savoy or green cabbage leaves
1 lb (450 g) Brussels sprouts, cleaned and trimmed
2 tablespoons walnut oil
1 large onion, thinly sliced
6 oz (170 g) chopped walnuts
8 oz (225 g) curd or ricotta cheese
2 eggs, beaten
sea salt and freshly ground black pepper
for the sauce
1 lb (450 g) tomatoes
¼ pint (150 ml) dry sherry
sea salt and freshly ground black pepper

Heat the oven to 400°F (200°C, gas mark 6).

Blanch the cabbage leaves in a saucepan of water and drain them. Boil the sprouts in a saucepan with a little salted water for 3 minutes, then drain and chop.

Heat the walnut oil in a pan and add the sliced onion; cook for 3 minutes until just soft. In a large bowl, combine the onion, walnuts, sprouts, cheese and beaten eggs. Season generously with salt and pepper.

Grease a 2½-pint (1400-ml) soufflé dish or mould and lay the cabbage leaves on the base and along the sides, leaving enough overhang to cover the top. Fill the mould with the mixture and fold the cabbage leaves over the top to cover. Place some buttered paper on top and bake in a bain marie for 45-50 minutes.

Meanwhile, make the sauce. Place the tomatoes with their skins and green stalks into a saucepan with the sherry and seasoning. Place over a low flame, covered, for 10 minutes. Then blend the sauce and sieve it. The resulting thin purée will taste superb with nothing else added. The tomatoes must have flavour to begin with but, at this time of year, they should have.

Remove the mould from the oven when it is ready and leave for 5 minutes to settle. Unmould on to a platter and pour a little of the tomato sauce around it.

LEEK, POTATO AND OLIVE GRATIN

Illustrated on page 51

─────── SERVES 6 ───────

2 oz (50 g) butter
3 cloves garlic, crushed
1½ lb (675 g) potatoes, peeled and thickly sliced
1½ lb (675 g) leeks, trimmed, cleaned and sliced across
½ pint (280 ml) dry white wine
sea salt and freshly ground black pepper
12 stoned black olives, sliced
2 tablespoons thick/double cream

Heat the butter in a saucepan and add the garlic and potatoes. Stir over a medium heat for a moment, before adding the leeks, white wine and seasoning. Stir, then cover and simmer for about 15-18 minutes. Stir in the black olives and the cream. Pour into a gratin dish and place under a hot grill, until the surface is golden.

GLAZED BEETROOT

Illustrated on page 51

─────── SERVES 6 ───────

1½ lb (675 g) small beetroot
2 tablespoons apple jelly
2 tablespoons water
sea salt and freshly ground black pepper

Boil the beetroot in their skins for an hour or until they are tender. Peel the beetroots and place them in a clean pan. Melt the apple jelly with the water and pour over the beetroot. Raise the heat beneath the pan, shaking it so that the beetroot are turned in the syrup. Season, pour into a shallow oven dish and keep warm.

AUTUMN · MENU 5

ROAST WILD DUCK WITH QUINCES

•

PARSNIP CROQUETTES

•

RUNNER BEANS IN TOMATO AND GARLIC SAUCE

I must confess that two of my favourite foods are the wild duck and the quince. Their combination in a single dish seems to me the height of gourmet ecstasy, akin to Sydney Smith's idea of heaven.

However, quinces are not easy to come by unless, like me, one is fortunate enough to have a tree, or you live near to certain of London's ethnic markets where they sometimes appear, unheralded, in late summer. If you live in the country, then quinces can be bought around October or November, at the height of the wild duck season. And if you have a garden and plant your runner beans late, you will then have beans when nobody else has. These, to my mind, are the best beans in the world. Instead of roasting the parsnips, I have made croquettes out of them — their sweetness goes well with game. These can be prepared ahead and then refrigerated before being quickly fried. Cook the runner beans just before serving time. This is quite an easy meal to organize.

As with the pheasant in Autumn Menu 3, if you use a heavy cast-iron dish, the birds will cook efficiently without getting dry.

ROAST WILD DUCK WITH QUINCES

Illustrated on page 54

—— SERVES 6 ——

2 wild ducks
6-8 quinces
5 oz quince jelly
3 tablespoons water
3 fl oz (75 ml) vermouth
sea salt and freshly ground black pepper

Heat the oven to 425°F (220°C, gas mark 7).

Place the two ducks in a large roasting bag. Season them with salt and pepper, and cover their breasts and top with buttered paper.

Peel the quinces, slice them in half, core them, and lay the halves around the ducks inside the bag. Close the bag, place in a baking dish, and bake in the oven in a heavy roasting pan for 1 hour.

Meanwhile, mix the other ingredients together over a low flame until they are combined.

When they are ready, remove the ducks from the bag and discard it. Put the quinces in another dish and replace lower in the oven, covered with the buttered paper from the ducks. Place the ducks back in the baking dish and pour over the quince jelly mixture. Return to the oven and roast for a further 15 minutes, basting every 4 minutes. Turn the ducks over so that, for some of the time, the breasts are cooking in the melted jelly. Remove the ducks from the oven and allow to set for 3-5 minutes before carving.

Serve with the roast quinces and all of the basting liquid.

Top: Wild Roast Duck with Quinces (page 53), centre, Runner Beans in Tomato and Garlic Sauce, below: Parsnip Croquettes.

PARSNIP CROQUETTES

—————— SERVES 6 ——————

2 lb (900 g) parsnips
2 oz (50 g) butter
1 teaspoon cumin
2 eggs, separated
1 tablespoon gram (besan) flour
sea salt and freshly ground black pepper
2 oz (50 g) fresh wholemeal breadcrumbs
butter and olive oil, for frying

Peel and trim the parsnips. Cut them into chunks, put them in a saucepan and boil them for 6 minutes, or until tender. Drain them well. Melt the butter in a saucepan and sweat the cumin for a minute or two. In a bowl, mash the parsnips. Add the butter and cumin, and the egg yolks. Sieve the gram flour into the parsnip mixture and combine it well. Season with salt and pepper to taste. Mix thoroughly and chill the mixture for an hour.

Put the egg whites into a bowl and beat to combine; spread the breadcrumbs on a plate. Remove the mixture from the refrigerator, pick off pieces from the dough and roll into sausage shapes. Dip them into the egg white and then into the breadcrumbs. Continue until all the mixture is used up. Refrigerate the croquettes until needed.

Fry the croquettes briefly in a mixture of butter and olive oil, so that the outside is crisp and brown.

RUNNER BEANS IN TOMATO AND GARLIC SAUCE

—————— SERVES 6 ——————

1 lb (450 g) tomatoes
3 cloves garlic, crushed
3 fl oz (75 ml) dry sherry
sea salt and freshly ground black pepper
1½ lb (675 g) runner beans, trimmed and sliced

Puncture the tomatoes and put them in a saucepan with the garlic and sherry. Season with salt and pepper. Place a lid over the pan and simmer the tomatoes in their own juice for 10 minutes. Push them through a sieve and discard the skin and pips.

Boil the beans in a little salted water for about 3 minutes. Drain them thoroughly.

Add the beans to the tomato sauce and bring to boiling point. Serve immediately.

AUTUMN · MENU 6

CASSEROLE OF ARTICHOKES

·

RICE AND PEPPER PILAF

In the autumn appear the magnificent globe artichokes from Brittany. These have huge pads of flesh at the base of their leaves, and it is not an extravagance to create a whole dish around them, as I have done here. They go particularly well with flageolet beans. In France at this season, one can buy the flageolet still within their pods, fitting them like ghostly sheaths. Basil is only just a seasonal ingredient now, for its life is almost at an end. We associate it always with tomato, but it is, I believe, a trenchant foil to many other vegetables.

Red peppers are in season at the same time. These are best if blistered and skinned, then chopped and added raw to the rice. Their juices lift the rice from a mediocre accompaniment to an exotic dish in its own right.

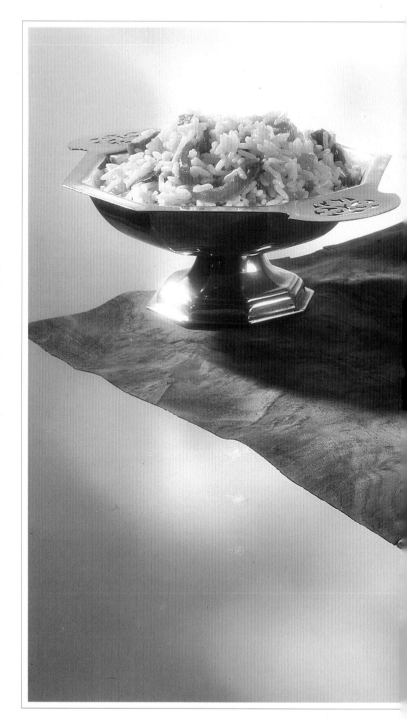

Left: Rice and Pepper Pilaf (page 58), right: Casserole of Artichokes (page 58).

56

CASEROLE OF ARTICHOKES

Illustrated on page 56/57

———— SERVES 6 ————

6-8 globe artichokes
4 oz (120 g) dried flageolet beans
1½ lb (675 g) potatoes
1½ lb (675 g) French beans
a large bunch of basil leaves
2 oz (50 g) butter
3 cloves garlic, crushed
1 oz (25 g) gram (besan) flour
½ pint (280 ml) dry white wine
sea salt and freshly ground black pepper

Place the artichokes in a large saucepan and boil them for 45 minutes. Drain thoroughly and let them cool. Tear off the outer leaves and scrape the edible flesh from the leaves with a spoon into a bowl. (This may seem a tedious business but it is more easily done than it seems.) Discard the inner leaves and the choke and reserve the bottom – if it is large, slice it in two or into quarters.

Soak the flageolet beans in a saucepan of water for an hour. Then drain them, cover with more water and boil for an hour, until they are tender. Measure out ½ pint (280 ml) of the cooking liquid to use as stock.

Peel and cut the potatoes into ¼-in (6-mm) chunks and trim and slice the beans into bite-size lengths. Chop the basil leaves fairly small. In one saucepan, parboil the potatoes for 12 minutes and in another the beans for 3 minutes.

Melt the butter in a casserole and add the garlic. Stir in the flour to make a roux. Pour in the wine and the reserved liquid to make a stock, then add the potatoes, French beans and artichoke bottoms. Cook for 10 minutes. Now add the flageolet beans and the artichoke purée taken from the leaves, and season with salt and pepper. Cook for a further 5 minutes. Stir in the basil leaves just before serving.

RICE AND PEPPER PILAF

Illustrated on page 56/57

———— SERVES 6 ————

8 oz (225 g) patna rice
1 large red pepper
1 large yellow pepper
½ lb (225 g) tomatoes, peeled and chopped
sea salt and freshly ground black pepper
1 oz (25 g) butter

Place the rice in a saucepan of salted water, and boil until tender. Drain, then dry the grains on a baking tray in the oven, at a low temperature, for a few minutes.

Meanwhile, grill the red and yellow peppers whole, or pierce them with the prongs of a fork and hold them over a flame until the skins blister and blacken. Scrape the skin away and slice off the tops. Core and seed the peppers, then dice the flesh small.

Mix together the peppers, tomatoes and rice in an ovenproof dish, season with salt and pepper to taste, and return to the oven for 10 minutes.

Serve with the butter just stirred in.

WINTER

Fresh winter salads tend to revolve around varieties of coleslaw. Red cabbage, green Savoy and the more traditional Dutch white are all good allied with onion or apple for a simple salad. Otherwise, mix them with citrus or dried fruits, julienne-sliced or grated vegetables, and nuts. Do not forget that salads can be partially cooked and eaten warm for cold days. Kohlrabi and celeriac, for instance, make a beautiful salad if they are sliced, briefly steamed and tossed in a tomato mayonnaise.

WINTER · MENU 1

WHITE FISH WITH CELERY, DILL AND PARSLEY BUTTER SAUCE

•

INDIVIDUAL POTATO SOUFFLES

•

BROCCOLI STUFFED WITH SLIVERS OF CARROT

•

HERB HOLLANDAISE

There is a variety of excellent white fish available in the winter and the fish dish uses celery and dill which combine beautifully. It is a fairly subtle flavour – complemented by the Potato Soufflés, which are also quite delicate – but the menu is enlivened by a simple Herb Hollandaise served with the Broccoli Stuffed with Carrot. The latter may run the risk of seeming pretentious but it cheers a menu that tends towards pale colours, and its crunchiness is particularly good.

All of these dishes can be prepared in advance up to the final stage. The fish can be cooked earlier in the day. Then, before the meal, the sauce is thickened and poured over the fish, and the dish is briefly reheated in the oven. The Potato Soufflés can be prepared beforehand and then baked in their bain marie at the last moment. The broccoli can be prepared and then just steamed before the meal. The Herb Hollandaise can be made earlier in the day.

WHITE FISH WITH CELERY, DILL AND PARSLEY BUTTER SAUCE

—————— SERVES 6 ——————

3 oz (85 g) butter
2½ lb (1.1 kg) white fish, such as cod, hake, haddock or sea bass, filleted and skinned
2-3 tender stalks celery, finely chopped
3 tablespoons finely chopped dill weed
a generous handful of parsley, finely chopped
¼ pint (150 ml) dry white wine
1 teaspoon celery salt
sea salt and freshly ground black pepper
1 teaspoon kuzu flour or cornflour, mixed with a little cold water

Heat the oven to 400°F (200°C, gas mark 6).

Use a little of the butter to grease an ovenproof dish. Place the fish in it, cover with a piece of buttered paper and bake for 10-12 minutes or until the fish is just done. Remove from the oven and drain off and reserve all the cooking liquid.

Melt the remaining butter in a saucepan, add the celery and sauté for 3-4 minutes. Add the dill weed, parsley, wine and fish cooking liquid. Simmer the sauce for a moment, add the celery salt and salt and pepper to taste, then add the kuzu mixture and stir until thickened. Pour the sauce over the fish and return to the oven for 5 minutes.

Top: Individual Potato Soufflé (page 62), below: White Fish with Celery, Dill and Parsley Butter Sauce and Herb Hollandaise (page 62), Broccoli Stuffed with Slivers of Carrot (page 62).

INDIVIDUAL POTATO SOUFFLES

Illustrated on page 61

Keep the two egg yolks left over from this recipe to use for the Herb Hollandaise.

──────── SERVES 6 ────────

1 lb (450 g) floury potatoes
2 oz (50 g) butter
sea salt and freshly ground black pepper
4 eggs, separated
extra butter, for greasing

Heat the oven to 400°F (200°C, gas mark 6).

Peel the potatoes and boil them until tender. Drain well, then mash and add the butter, salt and pepper. Allow to cool slightly, then add 2 of the egg yolks and beat until smooth. Whisk the egg whites until they form stiff peaks, then carefully fold them into the mixture.

Generously butter 6 individual ramekins and fill them two-thirds full with the potato mixture. Bake for 12-15 minutes, or until the soufflés are well risen and brown on top.

BROCCOLI STUFFED WITH SLIVERS OF CARROT

Illustrated on page 61

──────── SERVES 6 ────────

8-12 fairly thick broccoli stems
2-3 small carrots

Peel the tough outer skin from the broccoli stems and cut them into 4-5-in (10-12.5-cm) lengths. Using a small, very sharp knife, cut down the length of each stem to make a 'V'-shaped indentation to its centre.

Cut the carrots into the same-sized lengths, then cut 'V'-shapes out of them to fit the broccoli. Fit a carrot 'V' into each broccoli stem. Steam for 10 minutes.

HERB HOLLANDAISE

Illustrated on page 61

Although not a true Hollandaise, and it is served cold, this low-calorie sauce can enhance many vegetables, hot or cold.

─── MAKES APPROXIMATELY ¾ pint (420 ml) ───

2 tablespoons walnut oil
2 egg yolks, beaten
½ pint (280 ml) fromage frais, Greek yoghurt or quark
3 tablespoons freshly chopped parsley
sea salt and freshly ground black pepper

Gradually mix the oil into the egg yolks in a bowl – slowly add the fromage frais, stirring until thoroughly blended. Stir in the parsley and season to taste with salt and pepper.

WINTER·MENU 2

WILD DUCK BREASTS WITH BRANDY AND PEACH SAUCE

•

COUSCOUS PILAF

•

NAVETS A LA BORDELAISE

Many of us tend to despise the turnip as a vegetable. The French know better; they cook navets when they are very small. These baby turnips can now be purchased more easily, especially in large supermarkets. They go particularly well with game.

The duck should be marinated for 1-2 days prior to casseroling. It can then be cooked earlier in the day up to the moment when the breasts are removed. The best type of duck for cooking this style of recipe is the tufted duck. Though wild, it is a very common sight on city lakes and ponds. Its flesh has a stronger, darker taste than that of the mallard. Though a little tougher its flavour is unbeatable. If you cannot get tufted duck, use mallard.

The Couscous Pilaf can also be made beforehand and then steamed briefly for 5 minutes before serving. Its clean, earthy taste complements the game beautifully.

The shoyu sauce used in this menu and in Winter 3 and 4 is the Japanese version of soya sauce, made from fermenting soya beans — high in protein and with real food value. Another version is called Tamari. Both are available in Oriental shops and health food stores or sections of supermarkets. Avoid, if you can, the ordinary 'soy' sauces — made from chemicals, they have a harsh, bitter flavour.

Kuzu flour, too, is Japanese. Made from the root of an exotic plant, it thickens sauces in much the same way as arrowroot. But unlike the latter, it contains valuable protein, and so is particularly useful in a vegetarian diet.

WILD DUCK BREASTS WITH BRANDY AND PEACH SAUCE

Illustrated on page 65

———————— SERVES 6 ————————

3 wild ducks
1 bottle red wine
3 cloves garlic, crushed
1 onion, chopped
2 bay leaves
1 stem rosemary
sea salt and freshly ground black pepper
for the glaze
3 tablespoons apple or peach jelly
1 tablespoon brandy
1 tablespoon shoyu (Japanese soya) sauce
for the sauce
5 fresh white peaches, skinned and stoned, or 10 tinned peach halves in natural juice, drained
2 tablespoons brandy
1 teaspoon kuzu flour or cornflour mixed with 1 tablespoon shoyu sauce and 1 tablespoon water
for the garnish
watercress sprigs

Using a large heavy knife or poultry shears, cut the ducks in half along the backbone and place them in a large flameproof casserole. Pour over the wine and add all the other marinade ingredients. Marinate in the refrigerator for 1-2 days, turning from time to time.

Heat the oven to 400°F (200°C, gas mark 6).

Place the casserole over a moderate heat and bring to simmering point. Remove from the heat, cover and place in the oven for 20 minutes.

Reduce the heat to 350°F (180°C, gas mark 4) and cook for a further 45 minutes.

Remove the casserole from the oven and slice the breasts from the birds. Lay the breasts in a shallow ovenproof serving dish. (Use the duck carcasses and liquid in the casserole for a sensational game soup.) >

63

< Raise the oven heat to 425°F (220°C, gas mark 7).

Place the jelly with the brandy and shoyu in a saucepan and dissolve over a gentle heat, then pour it over the duck breasts. Return them to the oven for 10 minutes.

Meanwhile, make the sauce. Liquidize the peaches in a blender or food processor and add the brandy. Bring to the boil and add the kuzu mixture, stirring until thickened. Pour around the duck breasts and garnish with watercress.

COUSCOUS PILAF

SERVES 6

8 oz (225 g) couscous
½ small red pepper, cored, seeded and finely chopped
½ small yellow pepper, cored, seeded and finely chopped
½ small green pepper, cored, seeded and finely chopped
2 small carrots, grated
2 tablespoons olive oil
a handful of parsley, finely chopped
sea salt and freshly ground black pepper

Pour cold water over the couscous in a colander and drain immediately. Leave to stand in the colander for 20 minutes, breaking up the lumps with your fingers.

Meanwhile, mix the chopped pepper and carrots together in a bowl with the oil.

Tip the couscous into a steamer and place the vegetables on top. Steam for 45 minutes, then give the couscous a good stir, adding the parsley and salt and pepper to taste. Transfer to a heated serving dish.

NAVETS A LA BORDELAISE

SERVES 6

2 lb (900 g) baby turnips
2 tablespoons olive oil
3 shallots, finely chopped
3 cloves garlic, crushed
sea salt and freshly ground black pepper
a generous handful of parsley, finely chopped
3 tablespoons toasted breadcrumbs

Trim the turnips and cook them in boiling salted water for 5 minutes. Drain them and cut them in half. Heat the oil in a large saucepan and add the shallots and garlic, then the turnips. Season to taste with salt and pepper and sauté for 5-8 minutes, until the turnips are tender. Sprinkle over the parsley, then the breadcrumbs. Cook for a further 2 minutes. Transfer to a heated serving dish.

Top: Couscous Pilaf, centre: Navets à la Bordelaise, below: Wild Duck Breasts with Brandy and Peach Sauce (page 63).

Left: Nori Roulades (page 68), right: Gratin Vert (page 68). Noodles with Fresh Herbs (page 68).

WINTER · MENU 3

GRATIN VERT

•

NOODLES WITH FRESH HERBS

•

NORI ROULADES

Basically, this meal is a combination of pasta, vegetables, fruit, nuts and fresh herbs, chosen for its aesthetic and nutritional appeal in the winter months. I have long believed that pasta and vegetables go superbly together.

The roulades with their sea vegetable exterior and stuffing of fruit and nuts are a marvellous foil to the rest of the meal. They also look unusual and appealing. The nori used in the roulades is one of the most accessible sea vegetables. It is a Japanese speciality, and the sheets we buy here are processed there. These sheets can also be lightly grilled and crumbled over food as a condiment. Such sea vegetables are valuable sources of protein, far too often ignored in the West. If the roulade is made earlier in the day, it can be quickly reheated in the oven.

The Gratin Vert uses vegetables which are readily available in the winter and which need very little cooking. To get the best results, the gratin must be made just before it is served and eaten, since avocado is particularly temperamental. It must not hang around, for the flesh darkens easily in contact with the air. The noodles can be cooked beforehand and then tossed in the herbs and butter just before serving.

Serve each of the three dishes separately. Place the gratin and the noodles in different bowls, while the roulades can be sliced and arranged on a small platter.

GRATIN VERT

Illustrated on pages 66/67

Avocado is rarely eaten hot, but it can be excellent this way. It should only be heated, not cooked.

——————————— SERVES 6 ———————————

1 lb (450 g) broccoli
4 courgettes
2 oz (50 g) butter
2 ripe avocados
sea salt and freshly ground black pepper
2 tablespoons freshly grated Parmesan cheese

————————————————————————

Cut the broccoli florets from the stems, peel the stems and cut them into 2-in (5-cm) lengths. Slice them thinly and place them in a steamer with the broccoli florets. Trim and slice the courgettes to the same size and length as the broccoli stems and add to the steamer. Steam for 8-10 minutes, until the vegetables are tender but al dente. Heat the grill to high.

Melt the butter in a shallow flameproof or gratin dish and gently toss the vegetables in it. Peel and stone the avocados. Slice them and add to the other vegetables. Season with salt and pepper and toss again very gently, so as not to break up the avocado slices. Sprinkle with the Parmesan and place under the grill until the cheese has just melted.

NOODLES WITH FRESH HERBS

Illustrated on pages 66/67

——————————— SERVES 6 ———————————

Fresh, shop-bought pasta is now more readily available. You will need a good 1 lb (450 g) of tagliatelle to go with the gratin. You can also buy excellent wholemeal noodles (the Japanese ones made from buckwheat are especially good), which have a nutty flavour as well as being nutritious.

In the winter one also comes across fresh herbs as diverse as basil and coriander, as well as the more ubiquitous parsley. It is for you to decide how strongly-flavoured the noodles should be with the gratin. I find a mixture of finely chopped basil and coriander is particularly pleasant. Toss the well-drained cooked noodles in a little butter with most of the finely chopped herbs. Turn them on to a platter and scatter the remaining herbs over them with 3 or 4 tablespoons of freshly grated Parmesan cheese.

NORI ROULADES

Illustrated on pages 66/67

——————————— SERVES 6 ———————————

4 oz (120 g) dried apricots, soaked
4 oz (120 g) hazelnuts, ground
sea salt and freshly ground black pepper
4 sheets nori
2 tablespoons shoyu (Japanese soya) sauce

————————————————————————

Simmer the apricots in their soaking water in a saucepan for 10 minutes. Drain and process in a blender or food processor until reduced to a purée. Pour into a mixing bowl and stir in the ground hazelnuts and salt and pepper to taste. Mix to a paste.

Heat the oven to 350°F (180°C, gas mark 4).

Open out the nori sheets and place a quarter of the paste on each. Roll up, tucking in the ends. Lay the rolls in a shallow ovenproof dish and pour over the shoyu and 2 tablespoons water. Cover with a piece of buttered paper and bake for 20 minutes.

To serve, slice the roulades crossways into 1-in (2.5-cm) slices.

WINTER · MENU 4

SCALLOPS WITH GINGER AND HONEY

•

BUCKWHEAT CASSEROLE

•

CARROT AND CELERIAC PUREES

Scallops are one of the most attractive of all shellfish, with a delicate flavour which must never be impaired by overcooking. Nor can they be cooked before you need them. So, although this dish can be prepared in advance, the grilling should be done just before the scallops are served.

The more unusual cereals are flexible foods and go well with anything. They also make beautiful rice substitutes, which is why I have chosen to complement the scallops with the buckwheat casserole. It may be cooked beforehand and then finished off by reheating with the butter and the parsley. Serve the scallops in the gratin dish in which they are cooked, the buckwheat in an ordinary vegetable dish.

We are often unnecessarily nervous about serving a vegetable like carrots with fish, but this dish of two purées arranged in a spectacular, circular design looks marvellous on the table. The carrot and celeriac purées can both be prepared in advance. If they are reheated in the oven, cover with a buttered paper to prevent the surface from becoming dry.

SCALLOPS WITH GINGER AND HONEY

Illustrated on pages 70/71

—————— SERVES 6 ——————

18 scallops (allow 3 to each person)
½ pint (280 ml) fish stock
2 oz (50 g) fresh ginger root, finely grated
¼ pint (150 ml) shoyu (Japanese soya) sauce
2 tablespoons clear honey
butter, for greasing

First make the sauce. Bring the fish stock to the boil in a saucepan and simmer the ginger root in it for about 5 minutes, then add the shoyu and honey. Stir until the honey is dissolved.

Heat the grill to high.

Butter a large shallow flameproof or gratin dish. Lay the scallops in it, pour over the hot sauce and place under the grill, basting the scallops twice. Grill for 3 minutes, then turn the scallops and grill for a further 2 minutes.

BUCKWHEAT CASSEROLE

Illustrated on pages 70/71

—————— SERVES 6 ——————

4 oz (120 g) buckwheat
sea salt and freshly ground black pepper
2 oz (50 g) butter
a generous handful of parsley, finely chopped

Bring ¾ pint (420 ml) salted water to the boil in a saucepan. Add the buckwheat, cover, reduce the heat and simmer gently for 10 minutes, until the buckwheat has absorbed all the liquid and is light and fluffy. Stir in the butter and parsley and season to taste. Transfer to a heated serving dish.

CARROT AND CELERIAC PUREES

These are individual purées served together in a circular design. Start with a small portion of carrot purée in the centre and then surround it with a ring of celeriac purée. Surround that with more carrot and continue until both purées are used.

——————— SERVES 6 ———————

1½ lb (675 g) carrots, peeled and sliced
1½ lb (675 g) celeriac, peeled and sliced
2 oz (50 g) butter
¼ pint (150 ml) dry white wine
sea salt and freshly ground black pepper

Cook the carrots in a saucepan of boiling salted water until tender, then drain. Purée in a blender or food processor with half the butter and season well with pepper.

Put the celeriac in a heavy saucepan with the remaining butter and the wine and cook, covered, over a gentle heat for 20 minutes. Add a little hot water if it shows signs of drying out. Purée in a blender or food processor and season to taste with salt and pepper.

Left: Scallops with Ginger and Honey (page 69), Carrot and Celeriac Purées, centre: Buckwheat Casserole (page 69).

WINTER · MENU 5

SPICED BEAN
AND VEGETABLE CASSEROLE

·

RICE AND CHICKPEA PILAF

·

APPLE AND PEPPER PICKLE

This meal is designed for a cold day, to warm the spirits as much as the tum. You can always regulate the amount of spicy heat in your cooking by controlling the amount of chillies, whether they are dried, fresh or in powdered form. If you want this pickle to be very hot, double the amount of chillies and break them up to expose the seeds, though the amounts I have given for one small bowl will certainly make it pretty hot already.

The pickle is a stimulating contrast to the mild spices in the casserole. The latter will have a better flavour if it is cooked the day before and left for twenty-four hours before being carefully and slowly reheated. I particularly like the idea of combining the bean and vegetable mixture with a pilaf that has chickpeas among the rice.

Serve the pilaf upon a platter. A watercress and orange salad would go perfectly with this meal.

SPICED BEAN
AND VEGETABLE CASSEROLE

— SERVES 6 —

4 oz (120 g) haricot beans, soaked overnight
¼ pint (150 ml) olive oil
4 cloves garlic, crushed
½ teaspoon each whole cumin, cardomom, coriander, mustard and fenugreek seeds
1 teaspoon asafoetida and turmeric
1 lb (450 g) carrots, trimmed and sliced into strips
2 heads celery, chopped
4 baby turnips, trimmed and quartered
1 lb (450 g) leeks, cleaned and chopped
1 small cauliflower, broken into florets
½ pint (280 ml) red wine
2 tablespoons shoyu (Japanese soya) sauce
sea salt and freshly ground black pepper

Drain the haricot beans and put them into a saucepan with fresh cold water just to cover. Bring to the boil, then reduce the heat and simmer, covered, for 1 hour. Remove from the heat and reserve.

Heat the oil in a large flameproof casserole and add the garlic and spices. Stir and cook for a moment, then add the carrots, celery and turnips. Cook for 1 further minute, stirring, then add half the beans and liquid. Bring to the boil, then reduce the heat and simmer for 15 minutes.

Blend the remaining beans to a smooth purée in a blender or food processor and add to the casserole with all the remaining ingredients. Stir well and cook for a further 8-10 minutes. Pour into a large heated tureen to serve.

Left: Apple and Pepper Pickle (page 74), top: Spiced Bean and Vegetable Casserole, below: Rice and Chickpea Pilaf (page 74).

RICE AND CHICKPEA PILAF

Illustrated on pages 73

—————————— SERVES 6 ——————————

4 oz (120 g) chickpeas, soaked overnight
4 oz (120 g) patna rice
2 oz (50 g) butter
a generous handful of parsley, finely chopped
sea salt and freshly ground black pepper

Bring the chickpeas to the boil in their soaking liquid, then reduce the heat and simmer, covered, for 2 hours. Drain, reserving some of the water, and use to cook the rice. Drain the rice and mix with the chickpeas in a shallow serving dish. Stir in the butter, broken into pieces, and then the parsley. Season to taste with salt and plenty of pepper.

APPLE AND PEPPER PICKLE

Illustrated on pages 73

————— MAKES 1 SMALL BOWL OF CONDIMENT —————

3 tablespoons olive oil
2 dried red chillies
2 oz (50 g) fresh ginger root, peeled and thinly sliced
½ pint (280 ml) cider vinegar
2 large sharp dessert apples, peeled, cored and sliced
2 red peppers, cored, seeded and finely chopped
sea salt

Heat the olive oil in a saucepan and cook the ginger and chillies for 1 minute. Then add the vinegar and simmer over a low heat for 10 minutes. Add the apple, peppers and salt and cook for a further 5 minutes. Transfer to a small serving bowl and serve hot.

WINTER · MENU 6

STUFFED CABBAGE LEAVES

•

BLACK BEANS WITH GINGER AND GRAPEFRUIT

Here is a classic combination of flavours in this cabbage dish, with its stuffing of walnuts and curd cheese flavoured with coriander. It is reminiscent of the best cooking of Central Europe and the Balkans, whose winter dishes are most notable in terms of international cuisine. This is possibly because the people of these regions have more practice at cooking through long cold winter days than many other countries. I have, though, been geographically indiscreet; for as the accompaniment to this dish, I have borrowed a recipe from the West Indies, whose black bean dishes are the most exciting in the world.

The bean combination tastes better if made the day before and then reheated, and the grapefruit added before serving. The cabbage leaves can also be prepared ahead and then the final cooking completed just before the meal.

This meal need a fresh salad of leaves and it would be pleasant, in the winter, to choose something unusual and colourful. Try making a salad with curly endive and radicchio in a simple oil and lemon dressing. Serve the stuffed cabbage leaves arranged in a pattern on a large platter, using more of the curly endive as garnish.

Left: Black Beans with Ginger and Grapefruit (page 76), right: Stuffed Cabbage Leaves (page 76).

STUFFED CABBAGE LEAVES

Illustrated on pages 74/75

SERVES 6

---

18 green cabbage leaves (allow 3 per person)
the heart of 1 small green cabbage, chopped
2 oz (50 g) butter
10 oz (275 g) curd cheese
4 oz (120 g) chopped walnuts
1 egg, beaten
2 teaspoons ground coriander
sea salt and freshly ground black pepper
butter, for greasing

Heat the oven to 400°F (200°C, gas mark 6).

Blanch the cabbage leaves for 1 minute in boiling water, then drain thoroughly.

Melt the butter in a saucepan and cook the chopped cabbage for about 5 minutes, until soft. Turn into a mixing bowl and add the remaining ingredients. Mix thoroughly.

Divide the mixture into 18 portions, place a portion on each cabbage leaf and roll up, tucking in the outside as you do so, to make neat rolls. Place the rolls in a well-buttered ovenproof dish and cover with a piece of buttered paper and a lid or foil. Place in a bain marie and cook in the oven for 45 minutes, until the rolls are tender.

BLACK BEANS WITH GINGER AND GRAPEFRUIT

Illustrated on pages 74/75

SERVES 6

---

5 oz (140 g) black beans or black-eyed beans, soaked overnight
¼ pint (150 ml) olive oil
6-8 cloves garlic, peeled and sliced
3 oz (85 g) fresh ginger root, peeled and sliced
sea salt and freshly ground black pepper
2 grapefruits, peeled and segmented
a little plain flour
1 oz (25 g) butter

Drain the beans. Heat the oil in a flameproof casserole or heavy saucepan, add the garlic and ginger and cook for 1 minute, then add the beans. Give a good stir, then add enough water to cover the beans by 1 in (2.5 cm).

Cook over a gentle heat, covered, for 1 hour or a little longer, until the beans are tender. Season to taste with salt and pepper.

Dust the grapefruit segments with the flour, then fry briefly in the butter.

Drain the beans and turn them into a heated serving dish. Arrange the grapefruit segments in a pattern in and over the beans.

SALADS

A meal is not complete without a salad, however modest or slight. The palate needs the freshness and texture of raw vegetables alongside richer food, and nutritionally such a dish is also necessary. Only buy salad vegetables at their prime and as fresh as possible. (Poor quality cannot be disguised in salads.) Wash or scrub them thoroughly, but do not peel them. Try and find an efficient way of drying the leaf vegetables – nothing is worse than a watery vinigrette.

Some of the very best salads are also the most simple – a few raw leaves tossed with the right oil and vinegar dressing. Happily, more and more salad leaves are coming on to the market (the seeds are also easily bought to be grown in your own garden). Dandelion, rocket, radicchio, Chinese and Japanese mustard greens, as well as the many varieties of chicory, endive and lettuce are delicious singly as simple green salads. A mixed bowl with wholemeal bread croûtons is, to my mind, a feast in its own right.

Any salad is much improved by the addition of fresh herbs and edible flowers. Sweet basil, salad burnet, lemon balm, angelica, lovage, dill, chervil and golden marjoram add wonderful flavour and stimulus to any salad bowl. Nasturtium looks radiant and tastes peppery; try hollyhock, lavender and wild rose as well. All herb flowers can, of course, be eaten. Borage, for example, looks and tastes even better in a salad than it does on the rim of a glass of Pimms.

Fruit and nuts can do more than simply show imagination. They add texture as well as flavour. Perhaps we do not use enough fruit – a handful of berries or flowering currants lifts a leaf salad dramatically, while julienne green vegetables are excellent mixed with summer cherries and soft fruits. On the other hand, be slightly circumspect with nuts, scattering them sparingly, or in tiny chips, over leaves. They are also good ground and mixed in with a dressing. Always try and use fresh nuts – the difference in flavour is astonishing.

The last essential ingredient is the dressing. For a vinaigrette, make sure that the ratio of oil to lemon juice or vinegar is four or five to one. Use flavoured oils and vinegars – walnut, hazelnut or sesame oil and herb or fruit vinegars – including that made from the fermented Japanese umeboshi plum, switching the flavours to suit the ingredients. Bitter leaves can be balanced by adding a little honey to the dressing; the fresh flavours of green leaves heightened, but not swamped, by lemon and fresh herbs; runner or haricot beans perfectly complemented by a garlicky dressing.

Finally, always choose a bowl big enough to toss the salad immediately before serving without scattering leaves over the table or dumping them in your neighbour's lap.

CURLY ENDIVE
AND RADICCHIO SALAD

SERVES 6

4-5 dried apricots
¼ pint (150 ml) apple juice
1 head endive
2 heads radicchio
4 tablespoons olive oil
1 tablespoon lime or lemon juice
sea salt and freshly ground black pepper

Soak the apricots in the apple juice to cover overnight. Dice the apricots small and reserve the juice for drinking later.

Separate the leaves of the endive and throw them into a salad bowl and add the radicchio leaves to the endive. Make the vinaigrette. Just before serving, add the diced apricots to the salad, pour over the vinaigrette, season with salt and pepper and toss the salad well.

SALAD OF DANDELION AND ROCKET

—— SERVES 6 ——

1 heart of Little Gem lettuce
12-15 young dandelion leaves
10-12 rocket leaves
1 tablespoon white wine vinegar
2 cloves garlic, crushed
sea salt and freshly ground black pepper
4 tablespoons olive oil

Separate the leaves of the lettuce and lay them out in a large salad bowl. Sprinkle the other leaves over the top. Mix the rest of the ingredients together and, just before serving, toss the salad thoroughly.

SALAD ELONA

—— SERVES 6 ——

1 cucumber
½ lb (225 g) fresh strawberries
3 fl oz (80 ml) dry white wine
sea salt and freshly ground black pepper

With a fork scrape the cucumber skin away so that it is patterned in stripes. Slice the cucumber across thinly and arrange on a large platter in overlapping slices. Hull the strawberries and slice them in half – arrange these over the cucumber slices. Immediately before serving, sprinkle with salt and pepper from the mill, then pour over the wine.

ORIENTAL SALAD

—— SERVES 6 ——

4-5 Chinese leaves
3 oz (85 g) beanshoots
3 oz (85 g) mange-tout, sliced across, diamond shape
3 oz (85 g) mushrooms, sliced
3 oz (85 g) water chestnuts, sliced
1 head of celery, diced
1 green pepper, cored, seeded and sliced
for the dressing
1 teaspoon freshly grated ginger root
1 teaspoon finely sliced garlic
2 tablespoons soy sauce
2 teaspoons lemon juice
2 teaspoons sesame oil

Mix all the ingredients for the dressing together and leave for 1 hour for the flavours to develop.

Slice the Chinese leaves thinly and drop them into a large salad bowl. Add the beanshoots and the rest of the salad ingredients

Give the dressing a good stir and pour over the salad. Toss thoroughly before serving.

ALFALFA AND ORANGE SALAD

—— SERVES 6 ——

4 tablespoons olive oil
3 cloves garlic, crushed
2 slices wholemeal bread, diced
2 oranges
6 oz (170 g) alfalfa sprouts
2 oz (50 g) toasted almonds
sea salt and freshly ground black pepper
3 fl oz (80 ml) Pernod

Heat half of the oil in a pan and add the garlic and bread. Fry the bread until it is brown and crisp.

Peel the oranges and break them up into segments, ensuring that all the pith is removed. In a large bowl, mix the oranges, alfalfa, almonds and croûtons. Season with salt and pepper then, just before serving, pour over the Pernod and the rest of the oil.

GRAPEFRUIT AND PISTACHIO SALAD

—— SERVES 6 ——

2 ripe grapefruit
2 heads chicory
3 tablespoons pistachio nuts, shelled
3 tablespoons sour cream
1 tablespoon olive oil
1 tablespoon grapefruit juice
sea salt and freshly ground black pepper

Peel the grapefruit and take all the pith from the fruit. Chop the flesh coarsely and reserve the juice to drink later, saving a tablespoon for the sauce.

Lay the chicory leaves in a fan shape over a platter or arrange 3-4 on individual plates. Place a little grapefruit flesh on each piece of chicory.

Mix all the rest of the ingredients, together with the grapefruit juice, and pour over the fruit.

WINTER SALAD

—— SERVES 6 ——

2 tablespoons raisins
2 tablespoons lemon juice
2 tablespoons ground hazelnuts
4 tablespoons hazelnut oil
freshly ground black pepper
½ small white cabbage, grated
1 onion, grated
2 carrots, grated
2 courgettes, grated
1 cooking apple, grated
2 umeboshi plums, finely sliced
5-6 leaves from a cos lettuce

In one small bowl soak the raisins in the lemon juice for an hour and in another mix the ground hazelnuts with the oil, lemon juice and black pepper. Toss the cabbage with the rest of the vegetables and the plums in a large bowl. Pour over the dressing, add the plumped raisins, and toss the salad thoroughly. (You should need no salt because of the umeboshi plums.)

In an attractive salad bowl, arrange the cos lettuce leaves around the side and pile the salad in the middle.

INDEX